TOWARDS THE LIGHT

TOWARDS THE LIGHT

MAJA LISA ENGELHARDT

TWENTY CHURCH EMBELLISHMENTS

TEXT BY ELSE MARIE BUKDAHL

CONVERSATION BETWEEN CLAUS GRYMER AND MAJA LISA ENGELHARDT

PHOTOGRAPHS BY LEIF TUXEN

KRISTELIGT DAGBLADS FORLAG

THE DIVINE LIGHT AND THE HOPE OF RESURRECTION
MAJA LISA ENGELHARDT'S CHURCH EMBELLISHMENTS

God is light, and in Him is no darkness at all
(1.Joh 1, 5)

ARTISTS' INTERPRETATION OF CHRIST AS THE LIGHT OF THE WORLD

In the Western world, theology, philosophy and poetry have always occupied a more central position than the visual arts. Pictorial art has even often been seen as visualisations of ideas and concepts that were fixed beforehand. So it is not all that remarkable that church art has frequently been interpreted as a precise representation in visual form of the biblical texts and others relating to ecclesiastical history. However, the church artists themselves have always been aware that the word and the image neither can nor must ever correspond to each other exactly. In several cases the artists, for instance Caravaggio, even made independent contributions to the interpretation of the Bible and the history of the Church.[1] One of the very greatest of church artists, Leonardo da Vinci, the creator of the famous painting of *The Last Supper* in the church of Santa Maria delle Grazie in Milan, thus maintained that the language of pictorial art communicates knowledge that the word either cannot express in the same way or simply cannot capture.

The French philosopher Maurice Merleau-Ponty has interpreted Leonardo's wise statement in this way: The artistic insight is developed "via works of art that exist and which are visible in the same way as objects. It communicates itself through the works 'for all ages in the universe'. It is a silent knowledge that imparts shapes to works of art from things that 'have not been brought out of their shelter', as Rilke says with reference to Rodin; it comes from the eye and returns to the eye. We must understand the eye as the 'window of the soul'".[2]

Ever since Christianity took over the political and cultural scene in Rome, the outstanding artists who worked with church art have often asked themselves the following question: How is it possible to make visual that which is not immediately visible? How is it possible to visualise the sacred, the paradox of faith, the Trinity, the resurrection of the flesh, the coming of the Holy Spirit and life eternal? Especially artists who have instituted new departures in church art have had a sharp eye to the difficulty of capturing the Divine in a precise portrayal of a human figure or through other images of the world that we have always fought to rule and control.

Nave and choir
Gjellerup Church
Altarpiece and colouring

7

For it will often lead to the interpretation of the Divine being limited, indeed often being entirely determined, by our own thoughts and ideas. So viewers do not have their eyes opened to the fact that the Divine is that different thing that resides outside our sphere of influence and our reason – that which gives a new meaning to our world and reveals new perspectives. And this is exactly what the Risen Christ does.

Various church artists have chosen to visualise and symbolise the Divine or the Sacred through the abstract effects of which art is capable, primarily light. For light is universal. It cannot be grasped or captured, but it forces its way in everywhere and sweeps darkness aside. We can see and experience it; it is directly in front of us. It comes to us and pervades everything, but we cannot grasp and control it. It is in just this way that God's spirit and love permeate our world. They are always present but outside the sphere over which we have power. They create life, hope and meaning where despair and the dark shadows of death have otherwise reigned supreme.

Many of especially the best known church artists have not interpreted the Jewish prohibition of graven images as a straitjacket, but have simply seen it as a challenge and a precise expression of the fact that the Sacred cannot be visualised in human form. A sharper understanding of the special potentials and limitations of the pictorial idiom have ironically enough almost always appeared in connection with a fervent discussion of the aniconism expressed in the Old Testament. The violent conflict that was fought between those against and those in favour of images in the 8th and 9th centuries contains various interpretations of the original Jewish prohibition of images. It was those in favour of them who won. But the discussion that this conflict produced continued throughout the following centuries albeit in a less dramatic form, and it survives even today. The insight into the nature both of the Divine and of visual art expressed by the Jewish prohibition of images has time after time created openings in periods during which closed totalities and fossilised attitudes blocked the view and made it difficult to establish new rules for the creation of images.[3]

In the Byzantine mosaics that brought about a new dawn in church art, Christ appears as a flat, almost incorporeal figure that is often provided with a gleaming golden halo. The tessellae are arranged in such a way that they create an intense golden light and concentrate it in such a way that – both graphically and intensely – it can visualise the divine power and essence of God and Christ.

In Gothic churches, for instance the great cathedrals of Chartres and Reims, the stained glass is not there to provide light in the body of the church. It emerges rather as sources of light that has been inserted in the walls. It gathers the light and changes it and makes the windows themselves give out light. It is this mystical light and not daylight that fills the body of the church and transforms it into a symbol of the divine, for "the city had no need of the sun, neither of the moon, to shine in it, for the glory of God did lighten it" (Revelation

21, 23). It is the light in the Gothic church that combines architecture, sculpture and glass art into a visionary totality symbolising Christ, conceived as the Light and Saviour of the world

The monk Theophilus is one of the few artists in the Middle Ages to have described the view of art of his time, the central element in which – as in Byzantine art – is the creation of an expressive idiom capable especially of visualising the spiritual dimension and the paradox of faith. He emphasises that "God's Paradise", God Himself and the risen Christ can best be visualised through an almost celestial play of light and colour, through "the radiant splendour of the pieces of glass and the manifold qualities of the priceless craftsmanship" along with the variety of abstract elements of ornamentation.[4]

In their representation of God and the risen Christ during the Renaissance artists often resorted to sculptural techniques or paint registers that veiled the physicality but on the other hand reinforced the actual power of expression. When the church artists were bold enough to portray God, they sought to veil the directly human resemblance. For instance, Michelangelo's representations of God on the Sistine Chapel ceiling have neither physical weight nor a human face. God is enveloped in flowing garments, enclosed in an oval, and so He comes to appear more as an intense expression of creative power than as a person. Leonardo da Vinci especially made use of light to visualise God's divine power and love. He spoke of "the Lord God, the light of all things".[5]

But there is another aspect of the Christian message that has always challenged church artists' fertile ability to create images. This concerns the Incarnation or the fact that Christ demonstrated His unconditional love for us by himself becoming a human being and sharing our condition with us and dying the most painful death known in his time. So when artists are to portray Christ's life on earth they can make free use of their painterly skills and the countless intensity-replete registers and techniques for creating illusion that reside in the language of sculpture in order to give a vivid impression of the fact that during His time on our earth Jesus became a true man, but retained His divine powers and insights.

Even at an early stage, the monk Theophilus emphasised that when it is a question of Christ's Passion it is necessary to use an intensely figurative language in order to depict the way in which Christ showed His love for us by becoming a man who shared our condition in life and in death.[6] And we experience this in a very poetical and often imaginative way in the Romanesque and Gothic frescoes. During the Renaissance, when oil painting and linear perspective were introduced, the leading artists of the day, for instance Raphael, Titian and Tintoretto, could portray Christ's life and death with a particularly intense, expressive power. Christ's life and activity in our world were given immediacy in a completely new way. In the often very dramatic portrayals of Christ's life on earth during the Baroque, the viewer's imagination and feelings were introduced in a highly active manner.

During the 18th century, the philosophy of the Enlightenment led to science, art and culture becoming independent spheres that were no longer subordinated to the power and influence of the Church. This came to mean that the close links between Christianity and visual art were weakened and often directly broken. But both during this period and the following age the various representatives of the new period in visual art have often led to a renewal of church art and – through the eyes of their own time – provided new answers to how the Holy and the Divine can be visualised. Their works frequently contain traces of the insight into this subject originally acquired by the old masters.

In his biblical paintings, for instance *The Eucharist* (1909), the great Expressionist Emil Nolde made his figures flat, almost without physicality, and by means of his bold brush strokes, the strong colours and the suggestive contrasts between light and shade he has intensified the visualisation of the sacred act. In the chapel at Vence (1948-1961), Henri Matisse used the coloured light pouring in from the highly stylised stained glass to give a graphic impression of the presence of the Divine in our world. With convincing artistic force he has convincingly combined architecture, sculpture and other parts of the interior into a visionary whole that symbolises Christ understood as the Light and Saviour of the world. The great window in the southern transept of Cologne Cathedral, which was destroyed during the Second World War, has been transformed by the prominent German artist Gerhard Richter into a radiant, abstract, colourful area of stained glass and given the title of *4096 Colours* (2007). It visualises the Sacred in a contemporary optic. The light is "symbolical, but also quite tangible. It is the light landing on the coast of the world".[7] The famous Japanese architect Tadao Ando has actually called his church in Osaka *The Church of Light*. A cross in the apse directs a powerful, mystical white light into the dark church in such a way that we can see how the light of Christ forces the darkness aside.

Various Danish church artists have also found new artistic answers to the questions raised by seeking to portray the Divine. Among them are Per Kirkeby, Hein Heinsen, Jørn Larsen, Mogens Jørgensen, Bjørn Nørgaard, Peter Brandes and Maja Lisa Engelhardt, who over the last three decades – "in an outstanding and original manner" – have created what the art historian Mikael Wivel rightly calls a "renaissance in church embellishment in Denmark".[8] Another art historian, Anne Mette Gravgaard, has summed up parts of the Danish discussion centred on the problems relating to the visualisation of the Divine: "The idea of art as an expression of the Divine and the inconceivable, the sublime, is splendid and beautiful. The Divine can of course not be contained in a sculpture, but the cracks and fissures in the stone can provide a sense of transcendence, of absence and of longing for the Divine – the God who became man and who preceded us".[9]

That the presence of God and Christ is so often represented through a metaphor of light is very much due to the fact that Christ Himself told us in various contexts that He is "the light of the world" and so he that follows Him "shall not walk in darkness, but shall have the light of life. (John 8, 12). The life-giving power of love and the life-destroying character of hatred are represented by Christ as the contrast between light and darkness: "He that loveth his brother abideth in the light, and there is none occasion of stumbling in him. But he that hateth his brother is in darkness, and knoweth not whither he goeth, because that darkness hath blinded his eyes." (1 John, 2, 10-11)

Many of the solutions, both older and more recent, to the artistic interpretation of the Sacred and the Divine that have been brought out in this section serve to throw new light on Maja Lisa Engelhardt's church art and her representations of the Sacred and the Divine.

PRINCIPAL THEMES IN MAJA LISA ENGELHARDT'S CHURCH EMBELLISHMENTS

A multitude of artistic interpretations of the life-giving power of Christianity have always been characteristic of Maja Lisa Engelhardt's work. Sometimes this power has appeared in the form of discrete sunbeams in paintings of natural scenery. At others it has taken over her subject in a more pronounced manner. These two aspects can clearly be seen in her exhibitions in New York in 1995 and 1996. In the works from the first of these exhibitions, the Danish landscape emerged in the form of gossamer fragments in the golden light associated with the Danish Golden Age with discreet traces of inspiration from Johan Thomas Lundbye's landscape art. As Hans Edvard Nørregård-Nielsen points out, this very artist became "a true academy for Maja Lisa Engelhardt. The relationship had not least been expanded by the fact that with the same youthful reader's earnestness as Lundbye had experienced, she set about reading Kierkegaard in order to step into the magic circle around Christian things that encompasses not least *The Works of Love*."[10] In the paintings from the 1996 exhibition, the biblical account of the burning bush was interwoven into the natural scenery in such a way that it became a living, contemporary reality. We sensed God's presence, but we did not see His face. In both these series of paintings the divine perspective was made present through light and colour with a gentle reflection of the luminescence and the celestial light found in Niels Larsen Stevns's landscapes. The Danish hymns have also been a source of inspiration to Maja Lisa Engelhardt's church art. This applies particularly to the hymns of B.S. Ingemann, throughout which the light metaphor is a particularly striking feature, as for instance in "Radiant is light's angel".

Various Danish congregations have been fascinated by Maja Lisa Engelhardt's art and by the Christian message that lay more or less hidden in her paintings, and they have consequently asked her to provide

NOLI ME TANGERE
Acrylic on canvas, 1999, 100 x 78 cm,
Det Teologiske Fakultet, Copenhagen

embellishments for their churches. She has always undertaken her task with great respect both to the church building and to the congregation. To this can be added the fact that she has an incredible ability – both as an artist and as a human being – to reveal and enter into the various depths and the many layers that work with church art entails. She listens with all her senses open and she absorbs the church interior and its surroundings in her own self-forgetting way. But her final choice for embellishing the church is quite uncompromising. In her work on church embellishments she is very concerned not only with the embellishment of for instance the area relating to the altar and the pulpit, but also the colour of the church furniture, sketches for baptismal jugs, candelabra, chasubles and other forms of church craft are harmonised to the smallest detail so that they can be absorbed into a visual dialogue with the existing church and at the same time give it new perspectives and meanings.[11] Thus tradition and restoration are fused into an artistic whole that can open the way to a different and meaningful, artistically interpreted statement of the Christian message. In her studio at Colombes near Paris, she spends weeks, perhaps even months, working out sketch after sketch, finally to find the one that can form the basis of the new artistic whole she wants to create. During this long and often painful process, she finds that the picture comes to her – suddenly it is there. She focuses on the aspects of the message she considers the most essential, and which the painter, precisely the painter, can portray through the means at her disposal. As Merleau-Ponty has put it, she must "allow herself to be pervaded by the universe and not herself attempt to pervade it". For the artist must remember that "he lives in an enchanted world. He will himself believe that the actions that are most his own – the gestures, lines and strokes that he can achieve and which to others will be a revelation (…) derive from the objects themselves, like a pattern from the constellations. A change of roles has unavoidably taken place between the painter and what is seen. This is the reason why so many painters have said that "the objects look at them"."[12]

For Maja Lisa Engelhardt, colour is more important than form. It is very much indeed the vehicle for her expression. She is doubtless in agreement with Paul Klee when he emphasises that "colour is the place where my brain and the universe become one".[13] But the church's surroundings – whether an urban setting and a surrounding countryside – are brought in as landmarks for her church art. On the basis of a multiplicity of points of view she seeks to create embellishments that interpret those aspects of Christianity that she experiences as being particularly relevant or which have been overlooked. Her works contain many openings and fissures that allow the viewer so to speak to co-create. She has on several occasions underlined the fact that the aim of church art is primarily to ask questions. It neither can nor is intended to provide the ultimate answers.

There are especially two aspects of Christianity with which Maja Lisa Engelhardt has been very preoccupied and to which she has given visual expression in many different ways.

One of these is the range of problems described above. Maja Lisa Engelhardt provides several artistic answers to the question of how, in contrast to the God of the Old Testament, the risen Christ can become present among us without resembling the people we know. He comes to us, but we cannot see Him even though we can feel that He is there. How can this theme be given visual expression?

The other aspect of Christianity that has occupied her is how to give the congregation and other visitors a deeply expressive and contemporary artistic representation of the relationship between the Old Testament and the New Testament or the relationship between the Old Covenant and the New Covenant. If this aspect does not become visible in the church, an important foundation and an essential perspective in the Christian message will be missing. Erik A. Nielsen is right when he says that "*The New Testament* is in every respect un-readable and incomprehensible if we do not presuppose that its writings contain a radical, universalising and in certain respects 'wildly' spiritual reading of the world of concepts in *The Old Testament*".[14] We must not forget that the Church's first Bible was the Old Testament. The New Testament came later and it also became "a key to the right understanding of the Old Testament. For only when understood in the light of the belief in Jesus as Christ is the Old Testament part of the Church's Bible."[15] With Christ, a new light is thrown on the stories and images in the Old Testament. Maja Lisa Engelhardt is concerned with making these points of view visible in such a way that it becomes clear to Sunday congregations and other visitors that the foundation of the Old Testament is the law, and the Gospel's message of grace, love and forgiveness shines out over this foundation.

In most of the church embellishments that Maja Lisa Engelhardt has created, the artistic interpretations of these two themes – the risen Christ and the relationship between the Old Covenant and the New – are often brought together in a composition along with new colouring of larger or smaller parts of the church interior. So some of the colours that are vehicles for the expression, especially in the embellishment of the altar, are decisive for the colours adopted for the body of the church and thus play their part in creating not only a visual, but also a significant whole.

In her church art, Maja Lisa Engelhardt has never copied visible things. She has on the other hand worked on what Paul Klee calls "making visible what has been secretly revealed".[16] Her works in the various Danish churches are infused with an aspiration to make the Divine presence felt – not only in the actual embellish-ments, but also in the entire body of the church. So she would undoubtedly be in agreement with Johannes Jørgensen when he said that "art is a metaphor which seeks to express the eternal in earthly hieroglyphs".[17]

Tower porch
Grinderslev Church
Reflection from the south window

The visionary, spatial light in the church provides the eye, the thought and the mind with an idea and experience of what the word cannot express with the same intensity and also what it is impossible to grasp by means of figurative images from our world, especially the divine creative power and God's love, which cast a transfigurating light on our lives.

Maja Lisa Engelhardt created her first church embellishment in 1996 in *Øster Tørslev Church*, which is situated between Randers and Hadsund. The theme in the painting she chose for the church is the account from Exodus in which God reveals Himself to Moses in the form of a burning bush. The flames in the bush of thorns burn without consuming. Maja Lisa Engelhardt had treated this theme before. One day as she was painting it, something remarkable happened: "In the midst of the glowing red flames the crossbeam of a cross and a golden church tower appeared."[18] This vision was given concrete form in the painting for the nave in Øster Tørslev Church. Already in this work, Maja Lisa Engelhardt has pointed to the problems created by the portrayal of God and the risen Christ. We see the burning thorn bush, but not the Face of God – He is invisible. We see the cross and the church – but no precise portrayal of Christ.

Since 1996, Maja Lisa Engelhardt has created a large number of embellishments in Danish churches, where – from various angles and with constantly fresh emphases – she treats the main themes listed above: the relationship between the Old and the New Testaments and the depiction of the risen Christ. She has herself described three of her projects as a trilogy. These are the tasks she undertook in Skelund Church near Mariager Fjord in Jutland, Hylleholt Church in Fakse Ladeplads in Zealand and Frederiks Church at Alheden near Krarup in Jutland.

In *Skelund Church*, Maja Lisa Engelhardt has interpreted the relationship between the Old Testament and the New Testament in an almost sublimely dramatic manner and in such a way that it becomes strikingly present to the congregation. In order both discreetly and yet clearly to underline the fact that the Old Testament is the foundation, she has chosen to visualise one of its stories – Jacob wrestling with the angel – on the altar carpet. So, in a very visual manner it appears as a basis for the New Testament. For when the congregation kneels to receive Holy Communion – the bread and the wine that are the symbol of forgiveness – they look down at the Old Testament drama about Jacob wrestling with the angel.[19] As Lisbeth Smedegaard Andersen remarks, "Jacob's struggle with the angel is mankind's struggle with life and it is also the artist's struggle with her material."[20] During the struggle, Jacob received a heavy blow on the hollow of his thigh, which marked him for the rest of his life, but he did not let go of the angel. The story reveals that we never come unscathed through the often difficult struggles in life. In the altar carpet, which is woven in wool, silk, cotton, flax, angora and the odd silver thread, thereby achieving an intensely material effect, Maja Lisa Engelhardt has not retold the story. She has primarily used the contrasts between the cool greenish blue and the warm brown shades and

Chancel
Skelund Church
Altarpiece and altar carpet

16

the violent, almost spiral shaped rhythmic movements to visualise the violence and the pain in the wrestling scene. In this carpet, she has made use of no fewer than 138 different shades, and many of the threads used in the weaving are combinations of several colours. This increases the intensity and depth of the colour effect. But a few recognisable fragments of the Old Testament drama – the hip socket, which is painted in a powerful blue, and the angel's wings, which are characterised by greenish shades – appear and make the drama visible to the communicants at the same time as delineating boundaries between the visible and the invisible, between our world and the Kingdom of God. When the communicants rise, they see the altarpiece, in which the risen Christ, who has just met Mary Magdalene, comes towards them and becomes part of our world even if in reality he belongs to another world.[21] His body and face are completely hidden in a flowing robe that is modelled in bright green and blue colours that also characterise the landscape into which He is stepping. A circular move-ment suggests that He will soon be on His way up to his Father. We meet the risen Christ primarily in faith, and there He meets us. Through a dense and pastose layer of paint, Maja Lisa Engelhardt creates a vibrant life on the surface of her painting which together with the radiant light in the white tonalities makes Christ and His message of love and forgiveness present among us. In the image, it is just possible to sense a corner of His white shroud. This is a sign that death has finally been conquered. Mary Magdalene is not there – for it is the congregation that appears in her place to meet the risen Christ and the gospel which through the message of grace puts the legalistic religion of the Old Testament in a new light. For the new, simple altar, Maja Lisa Engelhardt has chosen to use the ashlars we know from our mediaeval churches, and which thus represent a reference to the Romanesque past of this church. In this way, tradition and restoration are fused.

The bright blues and the greenish shades in the altar carpet and in the altarpiece have determined the col-ours on the pulpit. The same applies to the colours on the backs of the pews. They are also painted in bluish greens and thus produce a totality of colour in the bright, white church. They almost have the effect of bluish waves, a reference to the nearby Mariager Fjord. The radiant, lightly sketched landscape in the altarpiece also makes the congregation think of the surrounding landscape along the Mariager Fjord. The blue and bluish greens refer to our world, especially to the landscape. On the other hand, the gilt on the altar rail and the small touches of gold in the interior suggest the Divine, which creates a new meaning in an often chaotic world.

In *Hylleholt Church* at Fakse Ladeplads, Maja Lisa Engelhardt has treated the two biblical themes visualised in Skelund Church from a new viewpoint that reveals fresh aspects. It is again only when communicants are kneeling at the altar rail that they can seriously experience the Old Testament motif she has chosen. This is the profoundly expressive story in Exodus in which Moses begs God to be allowed to see Him. God's reply is:

Chancel and nave
Hylleholt Church
Altarpiece and altar carpet

"Behold, there is a place by me, and thou shalt stand upon a rock. And it shall come to pass, while my glory passeth by, that I will put thee in a cleft of the rock and will cover thee with my hand while I pass by. And I will take away mine hand, and thou shalt see my back parts; but my face shall not be seen."[22] The account is ambiguous and so it contains challenges for the viewer. God's face is hidden, but His back is visible – He is present and absent at the same time. So Maja Lisa Engelhardt has visualised Him as a white, brightly shining cloud formation that appears to be passing by at the same time as seeming to be replete with His presence. Moses can just be discerned on the left in the altar carpet. He is standing on the cleft in the cliff, where there are contrasts between the cool blue and the shades of warm, dark reddish brown. They bring out the tension characterising the Old Testament story. And as Lisbeth Smedegaard Andersen remarks, the gold and platinum threads in the altar carpet help "underline the radiance, with the result that here is a carpet with a structure that lives and changes according to the light".[23]

Between the altar carpet and the altarpiece, Maja Lisa Engelhardt has chosen to cover the altar with a dark violet cloth that is decorated with a band of golden ears of corn. The dark violet shades in this cloth create associations to the reddish violet colours in the altar carpet and establish contrasts to the large area of shining white.

When the communicants look up after receiving Holy Communion and see the altarpiece portraying Christ's Ascension, they encounter a fragile figure surrounded by a cloud of strong white light that completely obliterates its outline. The light makes it clear that this is Christ, God's Son, speaking to His disciples for the last time before disappearing and going up to His Father, the Lord God. The artist shows how "Jesus disappears into and up in the cloud and thus vanishes out of our sight. This takes place against a background of a landscape vision rendered in cool, Nordic colours, pervaded and inundated with water, ice and fire."[24] The congregation is struck by the light of the gospels that the altarpiece radiates out into the church, and some will undoubtedly involuntarily think of the introduction to St John's Gospel (1, 1-5): "In the beginning was the Word, and the Word was with God, and the Word was God. The same was in the beginning with God (…) In him was life; and the life was the light of men. And the light shineth in darkness; and the darkness comprehended it not." Moses was not allowed to see God's face. Nor can we see it, but God sent Christ to us, and He is visible to us precisely through the word and the sacrament.

The lightly sketched and vibrant, warm brown and dark violet shades of Christ's flowing robe increase the intensity of the white halo which the light-filled cloud creates and with which it encircles Him while at the same time the great wealth of colours makes Him appear as a figure in a vision. What we encounter is a fleeting,

THE ASCENSION
Hylleholt Church
Detail of altarpiece, altar cloth
and the columns in the church

momentary image in a vast, indeterminate space. Christ is not body, but light. He approaches the congregation at the same time as he will shortly be on His way up to heaven. The light is drawing Him up. There are traces of all the colours of the rainbow in His clothes – gold, blue, purple. For there remain only traces of His life on earth. Behind Christ we see the outline of an angel – a sign that Christ is about to leave us. It is as though the interplay between light and colour is an event taking place in front of the congregation and other visitors to the church, and which they themselves are helping to create. The image of Christ is open and therefore has a powerful appeal to viewers. It is also they who determine whether it is Christ they meet. The image has no real beginning or ending. It is left to the viewer to complete it. It is placed in a Neo-Gothic frame and so is in the form of a triptych. The picture of the Ascension is surrounded by reproductions of poetical landscapes seen from a bird's eye perspective. They can be interpreted as "symbols of the Southern Zealand landscape",[25] and so the Gospel story is fixed as an event that is relevant to us and of significance in our local world and our everyday lives. Both during the Middle Ages and the Renaissance, various artists, for instance Pieter Bruegel, preferred to place the Bible stories in their own native surroundings. By doing this they wished precisely to bring out the immediate significance of the stories and their implications for ordinary people. Thus – in 1566 – Pieter Bruegel placed the account of the census in Bethlehem in a snow-covered Netherland town.

The intense light in the cloud formation in the altar carpet in the Old Testament world, which is seen "close to", establishes links to the expressive light in the cloud in the altarpiece, where the space is composed by means of a linear perspective with a vanishing point suggesting the heavenly regions. Christ's light provides a new interpretation of the Old Testament. Above the demands of the law, the Old Covenant, shines the New Covenant, which is the Gospel message of grace and love. The light shines on the congregation and other visitors to the church.

Maja Lisa Engelhard has decided on the colours for kneelers and the antependium, just as she has proposed the colours for the vault and the ribs, which are brought out in warm browns, earth colours. She has also ensured golden bronze for the carved circular motifs on the pew ends. Finally, she has coloured the capitals on the columns supporting the vaulting with intense reds and bright greens, which stand out bright against the white walls. The combination of colours gives the interior of the church a new profile and has been devised in such a way that it inspires congregations to turn their eyes towards the altar. In generally, Maja Lisa Engelhardt has succeeded in creating a new, light-filled whole in which is inscribed a visual dialogue with the elements that were in the church before she began her work.

In *Frederiks Church* near Karup, the artist has established a tense visual dialogue between an eventful story

Chancel and nave
Frederiks Church
Altarpiece and altar carpet

22

from the Old Testament and a dramatic text from the New Testament. The Old Testament story is that of how the Israelites carried the Ark of the Covenant through desert and mountain. When they struck camp, they built a tent and placed the Ark in the Holy of Holies. It was hidden from the people by means of a curtain. Moses tells how God had commanded him to direct the Israelites to make sacrificial gifts to him. They were intended to adorn the Ark.

The two artists who wove the altar carpet, Frédérique Bachellerie and Peter Schönwald from Atelier 3 in Paris, tell how they "built up a palette of over 100 shades of thread in various materials. It was a question of cotton, wool, flax, silk, alpaca, chinchilla, mohair, gold threads, metal threads, knotted rags, in some cases woven paper, and thanks to these materials we have been able to achieve the desired outcome."[26] Precisely the large number of powerful colour effects – especially the intense areas of gold and red – the golden gloss and the varied textuality provide a visual impression of individual aspects of the sacrificial gifts that Moses described with these words: "And this is the offering which ye shall take of them; gold, and silver, and brass, and blue, and purple, and scarlet, and fine linen, and goats' hair, and rams skins dyed red, and badgers' skins (…) And thou shalt put into the ark the testimony which I shall give thee. (…) And thou shalt make two cherubims of gold (…) And thou shalt make a candlestick of pure gold."[27]

On the altarpiece we see Christ tearing aside the curtain hiding the Holy of Holies in the Jewish temple. He appears in the picture almost anonymously and is dressed in a greyish costume, the outline of which is blurred by the powerful light. When resurrected, He is Himself the New Covenant. In the Letter to the Hebrews 9,15, this view is expressed with the words: "And for this cause, he is the mediator of the new testament that by means of death, for the redemption, for the redemption of the transgressions that were under the first testament". In the altarpiece He stands before us like a flood of light and gives us both blessing and grace. The fiery red curtain is painted with strong, rapid brush strokes that underline the dramatic event and create links with the red curtain around the Holy of Holies, of which we see a corner on the altar. As we approach through the nave it is as though Christ in the altarpiece is drawing us to Him and offering us His message of love. The altarpiece has been fitted in the old frame, which has not been gilded. But in the actual painting there is no silver, gold or any other precious object. Or, as Maja Lisa Engelhardt herself has expressed it: "The invisible God hidden behind the rich gift of the altar carpet now steps visibly forward and comes towards us in the golden frame of the altarpiece."[28] God asked the Israelites to make costly sacrifices to him, while Christ did the opposite. He sacrificed Himself for the sake of our sins, and with this the power of the Old Covenant has disappeared and the sacrifices have ceased.

24

THE ARK OF THE COVENANT
Frederiks Church
Altar carpet

When we look at the slight figure of Christ in the altarpiece, we have to think of Boris Pasternak's portrayal of Christ in *Dr. Zivago*. It runs thus: "The ancient world came to an end in Rome (…) Rome was a great market of borrowed gods and conquered peoples, a shop on two floors, one on earth and one in heaven (…) And in the midst of this orgy of tastelessness, marble and gold, the little Galilean appeared, clad in light, clearly human, demonstratively provincial, and from then on the age of the people and the gods was past, and mankind began (…) mankind, whose name sounds not in the least bit proud, mankind, rewardingly expressed in mothers' cradle songs and in collections of the world's paintings."[29] For Christ freed us from oppression and gave us human dignity.

Maja Lisa Engelhardt has also coloured both pulpit and pews, painting them in shades of grey set off by fields of bright, warm yellows. It is the greys in Christ's garments that have determined the choice of colours in the church furniture and created an overall effect in the body of the church.

In *Gjellerup Church* near Herning, which is the oldest dated village church in Denmark – it was built in 1140 – Maja Lisa Engelhardt has undertaken a very extensive restoration and renewal. Here, the congregation experiences a new and very dramatic visual dialogue between the fundamentals of the Old Covenant, in which God maintains the law, and the New Covenant, which proclaims forgiveness and love and introduces the Holy Spirit as an important element in the message of the New Testament. On the altar carpet the congregation encounters a fierce sea of flames in strongly contrasting colours that visualise the drama in Deuteronomy 4, 11-13, where "the mountain burned with fire unto the midst of heaven with darkness, clouds and thick darkness", and where the invisible God "declared unto you his covenant, which he commanded you to perform, even ten commandments; and he wrote them upon two tablets of stone." In the shape of a luminous silhouette covered by the green shades representing hope, Christ – in the altarpiece – steps out of the door and moves towards the congregation, proclaiming, "Peace be unto you."[30] Above the three panels of the altar there is a panel representing a radiant landscape which undoubtedly represents the Holy Spirit. Thus communicants meet God the Father, Son and Holy Spirit through fragments taken from the recognisable world and through a symphony of intense light and colour vibrations that make the Divine present and establish links with the yellow tonalities in the pulpit and the green and greyish blue painted panels on the pews. The green, which is the colour of spring and hope, creates an association with the Resurrection.

Maja Lisa Engelhardt has herself decided on these colours, which transform the body of the church into a light-filled whole opening the way to an understanding that the Kingdom of God is the kingdom of light, where everything is characterised by clarity and meaning.

Chancel and nave
Gjellerup Church
Altarpiece, altar carpet and pulpit

Maja Lisa Engelhardt has used stained glass in several churches to portray a selection of biblical motifs, primarily the Divine and the Sacred. Ever since the Middle Ages, church artists have captured these perspectives via various adaptations of stained glass and glass mosaic. For these art forms work with particular intensity with light and colour, and so they are as though made to visualise Christ as the "Light of the World", because they transform light into what could be called a "revelatory light".

If we ignore the achievements of the English artists during the Gothic Revival and the period when the Pre-Raphaelites dominated, stained glass did not occupy a place of importance during the 18th and 19th centuries. It was not until Jugendstil artists that stained glass acquired a new status. And several prominent modernists, for instance Matisse, George Rouault and Marc Chagall rejuvenated this art form in the 20th century.

In *Holsted Church* on the outskirts of Næstved on Zealand, Maja Lisa Engelhardt has created a monumental altarpiece in glass, measuring 6 x 4.6 metres, and placed it in a window made for it immediately behind the altar.[31] In this huge piece of stained glass, she has created a vision of "the Father of lights with whom there is no variableness, neither shadow of turning" (The General Epistle of James 1, 17-18). From Christ, who is standing with His back to us there comes a powerful, intense light that forces the dark sections back. Christ emerges as a dark, veiled figure, but behind Him there emerges a blaze of golden light which at the top finishes in a bluish landscape that opens up towards Heaven. At the bottom a red area emerges in which the visible brush strokes create a special form of life and motion. In this stained glass the light is no longer the daylight but is precisely transformed into a "revelatory light" that gives us an intense experience of the presence of Christ and of His love. The mosaic is transilluminated and so it contains the light within itself. It sends a coloured light – which both provides an experience and creates a meaning – out into space, into the space of the church. Maja Lisa Engelhardt has in particular taken as her starting point the text in St John's Gospel 14, 6 in which Jesus talks of His departure and His return. He will show the disciples the way to Himself and to God, but Thomas makes the doubtful comment: "Lord, we know nor whither thou goest; and how can we know the way?" To this, Jesus replies, "I am the way, the truth, and the life: no man cometh unto the Father, but by me." Mikael Wivel is right when he says that what we see "is this path of faith that Engelhardt has inserted into the landscape like a golden wedge. It emerges from the figure of Christ as he turns away from us and reaches right up to heaven. Like a clear metaphor for longing that stretches into space and sets the thoughts of the congregation wandering."[32]

The incredible illuminating power of the altarpiece and its remarkable, folded space is the result of a very complicated artistic process of creation. The work was – as Maja Lisa Engelhardt herself recalls – "created in

Chancel with altarpiece
Holsted Church

collaboration with Per Steen Hebsgaard and made with two layers of coloured glass: one layer of four milli-metre painted glass that was fired at about 700 degrees, and a layer of cut glass that has been assembled as a glass mosaic. This layer is made of mouth-blown, coloured glass, done under my supervision in St. Just close to Lyon in France". Through a complicated process of interweaving the two layers of painted and coloured glass they are surrounded by a layer of laminated and hardened transparent glass. With that process it has been possible to create a contemporary pleated light space that pushes the dark, flat sections aside and visualises the presence of Christ in an indeterminate place and in an indeterminate countryside – for the very reason that He is raised above time and place.

For this new church, Maja Lisa Engelhardt has created a baptismal dish with parts of the symbol of the Holy Spirit – the wings of a dove – in mosaic. The bottom of the dish is modelled in such a way that an ef-fect like that of phosphorescence is created when water is poured into it. The baptismal jug, too, is decorated with the wings of a dove. For the altar, she has created simple, cylindrical candlesticks that are decorated with a representation of the burning bush. The paten is decorated with ears of corn. The crown of thorns can be discerned on the chalice. These small pieces, all done in bronze, create points of intensity and unity in the church because there are connecting lines between the symbols with which they are adorned.

Grinderslev Church was originally an old monastic church. It is created in a very expressive Romanesque style and is situated close to Skive in Jutland. For this church, Maja Lisa Engelhardt has worked with glass art on a smaller scale, but just as intensely. For the two deep-set embrasures in the arched Romanesque style she has cre-ated two radiant stained glass windows. One of them turns south. The other is placed right at the centre of the church facing west. In designing the south-facing window she has started out from the elegant Romanesque cir-cular cross with intertwined ropes above the priest's entrance and a free-standing granite cross a few kilometres to the east of the church. She has also introduced references to the holy spring that once was a source of wealth for the monastery and the church. These inspirations are treated in such a way that the symbols of baptism and Holy Communion are linked together. In the west-facing mosaic the theme is "The Road to Emmaus", in which the light forces the darkness aside and creates a golden path. In both mosaics it can be seen how the artist makes the warm colours – the yellow, vertical formations and the red panels – vibrate by the use of blue.

The church and the surrounding landscape have stimulated her to allow especially the tower room to be pervaded with "the message of light" and a metaphysical light that she herself has described thus: "The light in the tower room, which is now no longer daylight, but a spiritual light created by the remarkable filtration deriving from the various coloured pieces of glass, I have thus attempted to make into the congregation's final

Baptismal dish
Holsted Church

experience on their way out, home or forward, after the service." In the church itself, the "message of light"[33] is suggested through the bright yellows and greys she has used for the pews.

The two stained glass windows that Maja Lisa Engelhardt created in 2005 for *Stoense Church* on Langeland show the extent to which colours change according to the strength of the light. These works stand almost like colour symphonies emphasising the simple Romanesque style of the church and visualising Christ as He who creates light in our changeable world with its many dark shadows, while they also establish communication lines with the metaphor of light in the church's ancient altarpiece. For the starting point for the altarpiece is precisely St Matthew 17, 5, where light plays a central part: "While he spake, behold, a bright cloud overshadowed them: and behold a voice out of the cloud, which said, This is my beloved Son, in whom I am well pleased; hear ye him." In this stained glass window, Maja Lisa Engelhardt has used double glass. This has had the result that the colours – especially the yellows – are particularly intense, while at the same time a fine sense of space is created. This is further brought out through a variation between glass that is mat and glass that is transparent. In the other stained glass window, where the white apparel and the red stripes refer to the woman he was healed of her issue of blood,[34] the same technique is used to achieve the impression of the actual drama in the story. The white area in the background was created in an opaque glass and therefore almost has the effect of alabaster and emits a very strong light. On the other hand, for the white garment the artist has used transparent glass. So the light shines through this and lights up the surrounding space.

Through their glass art, the old masters sought to make light sacred. Among them, for instance, were the anonymous artists who between 1136 and the end of the 13th century created the stained glass windows in the Basilica of Saint Denis and Chartres Cathedral, which was rebuilt in the 13th century after a devastating fire. They saw the colours, to which they attributed symbolical significance, as being more important than the narrative content.

Modern stained glass windows, in which there are only fragments of figuration, are particularly well suited to the Romanesque and Gothic Romanesque churches. This is because these works do not denote a striking new departure, but are organically inscribed in the architecture of the church and often even bring out its special character. The two stained glass windows that Maja Lisa Engelhardt created for *Kullerup Church* near Nyborg on Funen are in this way sensitively and discreetly absorbed into the Romanesque architecture. In a sea of varying strong light and intense, contrastive areas of colour, we find "The Burning Bush" and "The Vine" respectively in the east and west windows in the porch. "With the last rays of the sun," comments Sandra Kastfelt, "the west window summons people to their evening meal with its motif of a vine weighed down by bunches of grapes.

Stained glass
The west window from outside and inside
Stoense Church

An image of an evening meal in the twilight hour."[35] When the sun shines, various reflections are created on the opposite window and in the deep embrasures. Consequently, the porch is filled with a wealth of changing, vibrant colours.

For the east niche in the mediaeval Romanesque *Hørning Church*, Maja Lisa Engelhardt has chosen to devise a tessella-mosaic. The tessellae derive from Morano in Italy. They are fixed slightly skewed so as better both to capture and concentrate the light and to make felt the presence of the Divine. The shining green and gold tessellae produce an impression of the Tree of Life. Their radiance is increased by the gilt and silvered stones with which the embrasures are clad.

For the Catholic church in Frederiksberg, *Saint Mary's Church*, which is part of the Saint Lioba Convent, Maja Lisa Engelhardt has created her biggest and most monumental work in stained glass. The entire wall on the right of the very simple church is decorated with bright stained glass windows visualising the story of the Creation in a colourful, abstract idiom.

In the first window, which is on the far left, Maja Lisa Engelhardt has represented light as a fissure pushing the forces of darkness aside and opening up to a series of colourful, quite indeterminate formations that God has created on the first day. In the next window we encounter the firmament by means of which, on the second day of creation, God has divided the waters. This brings out the heavens and the seas in powerful bluish and greenish shades. The next window contains an almost labyrinthine network of stem-like figurations in radiant yellows and warm greens that receive further emphasis through patches of cool blues. This is the third day, when God said "Let the earth bring forth grass". Two big lights appear in an undulating sea of light that is pervaded by glowing, bright reds and yellows. The biggest represents the day, the smallest the night. They were created by God on the fourth day. Small living creatures, some yellow, some red, some white, flutter merrily around in a light-filled space. They represent God's joy at having created life on the fifth day, when He said, "Let the waters bring forth abundantly the moving creature that hath life, and fowl that may fly above the earth in the open firmament of heaven." Adam and Eve, whom God created on the sixth day, are seen in the picture as brown silhouettes surrounded by an intense yellow light. They are mirror images of each other and of equal stature.

All these stained glass windows, which visualise God's act of creation, fill the body of the church with a colour-saturated light. The final window, where God is resting, is on the other hand done in an alabaster-like glass and does not permit the light to enter, but rather creates a gentle white light and allows the outline of a church to appear – a discreet reference to the coming of Christ.

THE SIXTH DAY
Stained glass window
St Mary's Church, Lioba Convent

It is always the actual body of the church and its surroundings that have determined the kind of restoration Maja Lisa Engelhardt has undertaken in consultation with the congregation concerned. She has never omitted thoroughly and with great respect to analyse the history and appearance of the relevant churches before setting about making proposals for their restoration. The bodies of the churches have often required her to make very different artistic choices in order to establish a fine balance and harmony between tradition and restoration.

In *Mou Church*, which is built in the Gothic style and is situated in northern Jutland, it is the Protestant triptych altarpiece from 1582 that has determined the choice of colour and motif in the restorations proposed by Maja Lisa Engelhardt. The words of institution are written on the altarpiece in beautiful sweeping lettering of varying size. The warm red covering parts of the altarpiece refers to what Christ Himself called "my blood of the new testament, which is shed for many for the remission of sins" (Matthew 26,28). In order to emphasise the expressive simplicity of this altarpiece, Maja Lisa Engelhardt decided that a new altar in marbled stucco should be created, made in a brownish red shade and using the ancient technique. By means of light-filled, whitish yellow colours and silver threads. the woven altar carpet altar visualises the way in which, in Genesis, God "divided the light from the darkness" at the same time as shapes without any clear outline appeared out of chaos. So around the altar the creation of heaven and earth and Christ's message of reconciliation and forgiveness are interwoven and put into perspective.

In this church, Maja Lisa Engelhardt has sought to establish a unity of colour that both brings out its special character and creates harmonious transitions to the new features she has introduced. For – as she herself has put it – "the warm colours in the altar carpet are an extension of the colours in the altarpiece and are harmoniously linked to my choice otherwise of light golden colours in the church".[36]

Lodbjerg Church, which is situated in Thy on the northern side of the Limfjord, is rightly considered to be a "pearl of the Late Gothic style"; it stands surrounded by an undulating green landscape and enjoys a romantic view across the lake known as Flade Sø. It is the smallest mediaeval church in Denmark, and its small, but fine, expressive proportions have been brought out by Maja Lisa Engelhardt on a small scale through restorations that have their own special expressive quality. It was decided to retain the sensitive altarpiece from 1710, which was painted by J.J. Thrane and represents the institution of the Eucharist. It belongs to a quite different age from that of which we are part, but – in the words of Hans Edvard Nørregård-Nielsen – "in addition to much else it helps to make Christianity a living element in the cultural heritage that begins in Lodbjerg with the Romanesque font".[37] In order to turn the space around the altar into a light-filled area with a built-in

Altarpiece
Lodbjerg Church

drama, Maja Lisa Engelhardt has chosen to create two new side panels to the altarpiece. She has started out from the dramatic Gospel accounts of the empty tomb and the resurrection. As the minister of this church, Kaj Mogensen, puts it: "A closed altarpiece, a closed grave behind the enormous rock, which when the side panels are opened reveals what the grave contains: an empty tomb with a shadow of Christ disappearing – we must imagine – in a circular movement behind the old altarpiece – and coming into sight, transfigured and radiant in the right-hand side panel. He who went away is the same as He who ascends." (see p. 165)[38] In the left-hand panel there is a kind of shadow of an impression of the dead Christ, who has lain in the tomb. It is modelled in a negative form in black patinated bronze, surrounded by the bright space to which He ascends. In the right-hand panel He appears out of the darkness in a radiant positive shape modelled in golden patinated bronze. The five panels on the pulpit, which Maja Lisa Engelhardt has painted on a background of 24 carat gold, have been adapted to the proportions of the church and the character of the pulpit, while at the same time the artist has created small radiant areas illustrating essential biblical motifs. In the first of these, facing the chancel, the viewer finds the star over Bethlehem rising like a column of light above a landscape that is perhaps reminiscent of the undulating landscape surrounding the church. It is painted in powerful, sketch-like brush strokes that create life and movement on the surface.

The first time Maja Lisa Engelhardt saw *Vinding Church*, which is one of the oldest Viking churches in Denmark, she was inspired by her encounter with the Romanesque granite ashlars that are presumed to represent Jacob asleep with his head on a boulder. She herself has described this meeting as follows: "The wonderful Romanesque granite sculpture with a Jacob who is surely sleeping and dreaming, is so much part of the church and so integral to the attentive parishioner's memory, that from the very beginning I was inspired by its aura and its meaning. Like so many of our ancient churches, this church stands on a hill, and already here in his dream Jacob is helped up towards God."[39] It was another hill that became the starting point for the altarpiece in the church, that is to say Mount Tabor, where Christ appears radiant and transfigured. He seems to be part of the heavens and the clouds. (See p. 152)[40] Maja Lisa Engelhardt has had the altar made in different shades of granite in order to create a link with the ashlar and the sleeping figure of Jacob.

On walking up the nave in *Turup Church* near Assens, where Maja Lisa Engelhardt undertook an extensive restoration in 2007, we find a brilliant white Gothic church in which the altarpiece portraying Christ on the shores of the lake appears to come towards us in love and forgiveness. He appears as a figure created by light.[41]

Both in this and in others of Maja Lisa Engelhardt's altarpieces there is a characteristic feature, which Nils Ohrt has described in these words: "As strong as a column and soft as a shadow, the unfathomable Christ stands

Romanesque granite sculpture
Vinding Church

on the borderline between our space and that of the image, part this world and part the world to come, and is replete with the same multiplicity of meanings as Maja Lisa Engelhardt's art itself."[42]

Maja Lisa Engelhardt has primarily created new embellishments – often quite new, radiant naves – in some of the glorious array of Romanesque and Gothic village churches that are such a characteristic feature in the history of Danish culture and art. But *Saint Catherine's Church* in Ribe is a large and monumental monastic church. This is probably the reason why she has chosen the dramatic Old Testament account of the burning bush as the motif for both the altar carpet and for a large painting in the nave. For this story is one of great force. The sea of flames shines in the church. It creates new life and dramatic features in the great church. It also reminds us – as Jørgen Bork Hansen remarks – that 'the juniper bush, the nature she sees, points to the invisible. That is to say God. What is visible tells us of what is invisible. We find this thought, too, in Kierkegaard in *The Works of Love*: "I believe that the visible has been created by that which is not seen; I see the world, but I do not see the invisible. I believe it."'[43]

In most of the churches that Maja Lisa Engelhardt has embellished and otherwise restored, she has concentrated in the area around the altar. But in *Skannerup Church* near Skanderborg she has at the exit placed a small painting of Christ that stands there as a vision permeated with a golden light. This painting acts as a farewell greeting – an expression of gratitude for the insight and inspiration that the Divine Service has given.

NOTES

1 Else Marie Bukdahl, "Billedkunstens betydningsskabende kraft. Caravaggios *Kristi gravlæggelse* in *Hvorfor kunst*, edited by Lisbeth Bonde and Maria Fabricius Hansen, Copenhagen 2007, pp, 47-49.

2 Maurice Merlau-Ponty, *Maleren og filosoffen*, Copenhagen 1970, p. 54. Translated from the Danish version by Laurits Lauritsen of L'œil et l'esprit, Paris, 1961. The quotations from Leonardo da Vinci derive from Robert Delaunay's book *Du cubisme à l'art abstrait*, Paris 1957. See also Rainer Maria Rilke, *Auguste Rodin*, Paris 1928, p. 150.

3 See for instance Else Marie Bukdahl, "Kierkegaards kritik af kirkekunsten" in *At være sig selv nærværende – festskrift til Niels Jørgen Cappelørn*, edited by Joaakim Garff, Ettore Rocca and Pia Søltoft, Copenhagen 2010, pp. 180-200.

4 The quotations are from his famous *De Diversis Artibus* from c. 1120.

5 Leonardo da Vinci, *Notebooks*.

6 See Note 4.

7 Anders Ehlers Dam, "Lysmetafysik", *Weekendavisen*, no. 12, 2008.

8 Mikael Wivel, *Kunsten i kirken, Danske kirkeudsmykninger fra de sidste hundrede år*, Copenhagen 2005, p. 7.

9 Anne-Mette Gravgaard, *Tro – Rum – Billede. Kunst i kirken. Overvejelser og eksempler*, Århus 2002, p. 36. Especially Hein Heinsen has argued strongly that the abstract effects, primarily light, are particularly suited to visualising the Divine. Poul Erik Tøjner has expressed himself in the same vein (op. cit., p. 36).

10 Hans Edvard Nørregård-Nielsen, "Under ledestjernen" in the catalogue accompanying the exhibition *Åbenbaret. Maja Lisa Engelhardt*, Museet for Religiøs Kunst, Lemvig 2004, p. 39.

11 More aspects of Maja Lisa Engelhardt's church embellishments and the chasubles she has created are considered by Sandra Kastfelt, Hans Edvard Nørregård-Nielsen and Niels Ohrt in the catalogue accompanying the exhibition *Åbenbaret. Maja Lisa Engelhardt*, Museet for Religiøs Kunst, Lemvig, Nivaagaards Malerisamling and Kunsthallen Brandts Klædefabrik, 2004-2005. The catalogue is richly illustrated.

12 See also Maurice Merleau-Ponty, *op. cit.* pp. 25-26.

13 Will Grohmann, *Paul Klee*, Paris 1954, p. 141. This quotation is also carried by Merleau-Ponty, op. cit, 46.

14 Erik A. Nielsen, *Kristendommens retorik. Den kristne digtnings billedformer*, Copenhagen 2009, p. 275.

15 Lisbeth Kjær Müller and Mogens Müller, *Bogen om Bibelen*, Copenhagen 2004. p. 367.

16 Paul Klee, *Om moderne kunst*, Copenhagen 1964, p. 26.

17 *Taarnet*, no. 2, December 1893, p. 55.

18 Sandra Kastfelt, "Maja Lisa Engelhardts kirkeudsmykninger", in *Åbenbaret, op. cit.*, p. 13.

19 The account of Jacob wrestling with the angel is in Genesis, Chapter 32.

20 Lisbeth Smedegaard Andersen, "Usynlig til synlig" in *Maja Lisa Engelhardt. Usynlig til synlig. Fra Det Gamle til Det Nye Testamente*. Museet i Holmen – Løgumkloster 2002, p.7.

21 The motif of the altarpiece, "Noli me tangere – Touch me not" derives from St John's Gospel 20, 19.

22 Exodus 33, 21-23.

23 Lisbeth Smedegaard Andersen, "Det skjulte og det åbenbarede" in *Hylleholt Kirke*, Fakse Ladeplads 2002, p. 28.

24 Henrik Wivel, *Maja Lisa Engelhardt. En monografi*, Copenhagen 2002, p. 307.

25 Lisbeth Smedegaard Andersen, *op. cit.*, p. 25.

26 Frédérique Bachellerie and Peter Schönwald, "En Dobbelthed" in *Frederiks Kirke – Alheden*, Karup 2003, p. 10.

27 Exodus 25, 3-5, 16, 18 31.

28 Maja Lisa Engelhardt, "Den ny pagt" in *Frederiks Kirke*, Karup 2003, p. 15.

29 Boris Pasternak, *Dr Zivago*, Copenhagen 1958, p. 50.

30 John 20, 19.

31 During the building of Holsted Church Maja Lisa Engelhardt worked together with the architect and the congregation, and so it was possible to create a place that was particularly suited to this very large creation in stained glass.

32 Mikael Wivel, *Kunsten i kirken*, Copenhagen 2005, p.190.

33 Maja Lisa Engelhardt, "Om den nye udsmykning" in *Grinderslev Kirke*, Skive 2001, p. 15.

34 Mark 5, 25-35.

35 Sandra Kastfelt, "Bag Guds hånd. Maja Lisa Engelhardts kirkeudsmykninger" in *Åbenbaret. Maja Lisa Engelhardt*, Lemvig 2004, p. 24.

36 Maja Lisa Engelhardt, "Nyt altartæppe, alterskranke og farvesætning, *Mou Kirke*, 2008, p. 5.

37 Hans Edvard Nørregård-Nielsen, "Lodbjerg" in *Sognenyt*, no. 4, 2009, p. 14.

38 Kaj Mogensen, "Farvesætning og ny udsmykning" in *Lodbjerg Kirke*, Lodbjerg Menighedsråd, 2009, p. 20.

39 *Vinding Kirke*, an unpublished note made by Maja Lisa Engelhardt.

40 The text that inspired Maja Lisa Engelhardt is to be found in Matthew 17, 1-8.

41 The inspiration for this altarpiece is the story of the miraculous draft of fishes, Luk 4,5-11.

42 Nils Ohrt, "Naturens spor" in *Åbenbaret. Maja Lisa Engelhardt*. Lemvig, 2004, p. 10.

43 Jørgen Bork Hansen, "Den brændende tornebusk. Maja Lisa Engelhardts altertæppe til Sct. Catharinæ Kirke i Ribe", Ribe 2005, p. 14.

Maja Lisa Engelhardt. Lodbjerg Church 2009

LIFE, FAITH AND WORKS

I.

My parents had a dreadful life together. I had sometimes quite literally to put myself between them to prevent their equally literally coming to blows. They were simply incapable of communicating. That was often done through me. My mother could be terribly aggressive and quite terrible, violent and directly revolting in her need for alcohol. As a child, you become terribly afraid at this. Also because you haven't anywhere to go. You feel that everything can disappear. It's very difficult for a child to know what is right in that situation. You don't know how best to help when your mother wants you to go out and buy drink for her. You don't know whether the right thing is to do as you are told. Or whether the right thing is *not* to do as you are told. There you stand, a twelve-year-old girl with no idea what to do. Worst of all for me as a child was this very doubt as to whether what I was doing was right. But I never talked to anyone else about it.

My mother sat there with a razor blade in her hand. Threatening. And it was not only herself she was threatening, but me as well. She would say, "Maja, if you don't do it, then it's your fault". Meaning that I must realise of the consequences if I didn't fetch some drink for her. In that case, my mother, who was an alcoholic, would commit suicide.

This glimpse of the razor blade and death is also a glimpse of the reality that that was mine during my childhood in western Zealand. I was born in Frederiksberg in 1956, but after some years, my parents, Knud Harald Jensen and Elli Rasmussen, decided that our little family should settle in Sweden. This was in Bohuslän close to the coast, an archipelago environment to the north west of Gothenburg. My father was a trained draughtsman, but he was without a permanent job. And in general he had no fixed job. He never finished anything. All he had were diffuse and non-committal ideas about a different way of life.

In 1960, we moved back to Denmark, this time going to live 10 kilometres north of Kalundborg, between Saltbæk and Lille Vrøj, once the site of a lock, but no more. Here, my parents rented a smallholding which like the place in Sweden was close to the sea. In time, my two sisters were born, four and ten years younger than I. They became both a burden and a gift to me. Even by the age of ten I understood that I would have to accept responsibility for my sisters and in general for everyday life in the little smallholding. It was so to speak me or chaos. The very close relationship between us three girls was the fixed point in a family that otherwise had no fixed point.

THE BURNING BUSH
Acrylic on canvas, 1995, 200 x 340 cm
Vor Frue Kloster, Helsingør

44

45

You never knew what to expect of my father. As time went on, there was virtually nothing to be expected of my mother; she resigned and disappeared into her own world, comforting herself with alcohol.

When things were worst with my mother, I turned to God. Summoning up all my childish strength, I prayed to Him to help me to act as I should. Prayer gave me strength. I was convinced – in the naive way that a 12-year-old can be – that God was keeping an eye on everything we did. It ended with my deciding to give my mother what she asked for. So I went across and knocked on the crabby grocer's door. "Oh, your mother's at it again," was all he said. In spite of the hurt I received in this way, I felt that the kindest thing I could do was to buy the drink she wanted so that she could again withdraw into her drunken stupor and lose a sense of where and who she was. When she later sobered up, she always promised to improve her ways. But it only lasted a short time, and then she was off again.

I prayed that God would forgive me if what I was doing was wrong. But I couldn't do otherwise. I couldn't accept responsibility for her perhaps taking her own life if I refused to get hold of drink for her. As a child, you are in the power of the grown-ups. And I never defied my mother. I hadn't the heart. In principle, of course, I could simply have left her to her own devices. But I couldn't bring myself to do that. I saw a human being in need. I heard a cry for help. And I couldn't ignore that. Neither as a child nor since have I been able to ignore such a cry. With that baggage, I virtually never experienced what it is to be a child. I always had a responsibility. At the same time I always wanted to keep control of myself. I would never do anything that I didn't like. I didn't want to go to school dances, and in general I didn't go to parties. My school friends started drinking beer and smoking. I wouldn't do that either. So I made fun of it instead. Everything I didn't want to take part in, I made fun of.

Deep down inside me, I have always had someone who shared my secret and kept a check on me. If I said something stupid, I never avoided being confronted with it. At the bottom of my heart. I grumbled at myself if I had said or done anything stupid. And I was surprised at how others could behave as they did without it's apparently being of any significance for them. I have never taken the liberty of doing anything with the excuse that I was only a child. In that way, I have never been a grown up. As far back as I can remember, I have thought about what I could and could not do. There was no one else to tell me. I was never told how to behave. In reality, I could do as I wanted. For instance, I could simply have stayed at home from school. My parents wouldn't have protested. They didn't care. And it was I who was responsible for getting my sisters to school. Some people might perhaps think it was lovely that my parents never interfered. But it was dreadful.

THE BURNING BUSH
Acrylic on canvas, 1995, 200 x 340 cm
Vor Frue Kloster, Helsingør

2

So it was impossible for me to reckon with my parents, the two people who should have been closest to me. But I could reckon with nature. I went out into it when staying at home was intolerable. The infinite space there became a life-giving contrast to the claustrophobia of everyday life. Help in need. I sought the area around Saltbæk Bay which has been declared an area of outstanding natural beauty. There I could exclude everything else. Perhaps I was only out there for an hour or so. But then I had again gathered strength again to bear the unbearable.

When I was afraid, restless or upset, I went out into nature. There, I encountered the fantastic force there is for instance in the sea. At the same time I sensed that there was something behind all this. Some order behind the progression of the seasons, indeed a cohesion right down to the smallest detail. It meant something to me to sense that there was a force of this kind holding everything together.

Ever since the time when I was quite a small girl, I had been deeply fascinated by nature and I drew and painted what I saw. When I sat with a flower and looked at it closely, I thought, "Who has decided that where should be all those colours?" I was fascinated by the diversity and the light there is in nature. When I saw a rainbow, when I looked out across the sea or when I looked at the clouds and the colours at sunset or sunrise – well, then I thought of the power there had to be behind it all. I simply couldn't imagine that nature had created itself. There had to be something that had started it all and something that had an overall view of it all. As far back as I can remember, I have thought there must be a god behind it all. But I didn't dare approach that god. I got no help from my parents and their friends. They talked about some Indian gurus but I simply couldn't relate to them. Perhaps Christ was in reality just a guru. I was afraid in believing in something that was wrong. And so I dared not believe in Christ. I was 16 or 17 when I seriously started thinking about Christianity.

Then Kierkegaard caught me. He was the greatest turning point in my life. His *Christian Discourses* and *The Works of Love* are the two books that mean most of all to me. When Kierkegaard writes of the single individual, I feel myself to be that single individual. He speaks to me in a quite contemporary manner; he has opened faith to me and helped me to the trust that is necessary if we are to put aside fear and distrust. In my eyes, Kierkegaard is the greatest priest. And I read him every day. I always have him with me. He is the guide who makes clear to me the texts in the Old and the New Testaments. Just as he in general reveals Christianity to me.

It was *The Works of Love* that revealed Christianity as a whole to me. Precisely Christianity and not religion

Monotypes
B.S. Ingemann's Songs for
Morning and Evening
Illustrations, 2008, 42 x 31 cm
Private Collection

in broad and general terms. Religion can consist of many spiritual movements, none of which are necessarily Christian. But from Kierkegaard I learned that I was a Christian. He gave me the courage and the strength – and this is something for which I must thank him – to take the step to believing.

Everything is for your best when you believe, says Kierkegaard. And I feel no bitterness for what I have been through, and nor have I ever done. I tried to do what I had to do. I viewed it all to be jobs to be seen to. That, too, has played its part in cleansing me. Incidentally, I have never had a specific dream regarding my life, not even the dream of becoming an artist. On the other hand, I have had a longing for God, and there is nothing that means more for me than this longing. This forms the basis of my work. The longing for God is also the longing for life, for goodness, for eternity. And for belonging together with something. To feel that I exist in God's eyes gives me the greatest feeling of peace I know. I feel a great sense of duty towards other people, a duty to help them where I can. But the most fundamental is that I primarily belong to God.

3.

I had my first exhibition in 1985 with a series of paintings called "Klædebon" ("Raiment") in the Nikolaj Exhibition Hall in Copenhagen. The world of Christian motifs was right from the start a significant source of inspiration to me. The title of these first paintings to be shown in public derives from the story in St Matthew's Gospel about the women standing by the grave on Easter morning. The text says of the angel who overturned the stone to the tomb: "His countenance was like lightning, and his raiment white as snow".

I was fascinated at an early stage by the Golden Age painter Johan Thomas Lundbye, and so I still am. When I came across his name for the first time, I must have been 14 or 15 years old, and I was fascinated by this great artist, who came from the area where I had spent my childhood. I visited the house in Kalundborg in which he had lived and also the places in the landscape where he had found some of his motifs.

I feel that there are various things that create a link between me and Lundbye. For instance, he was a Christian. And he was also taken by Søren Kierkegaard. And like me, he longed for beauty. For goodness. He died at the age of only 29, whereas I had had reached that age before I seriously started to paint.

After taking the Middle School Examination from Kalundborg High School in 1971, I earned some money by taking various odd jobs for a few years. This was money that was to enable me to take the path that was the only right one for me. And then I went to the art high school in Holbæk. My parents were not well off and so couldn't give me any financial support for my training. But I so much wanted to go to an art high school.

Raiment
Acrylic on canvas, 1985, 146 x 114 cm
Private Collection

And it was fantastic that it was possible to get a grant to attend one. I was in Holbæk for the six months the course lasted. After that I did six months in an art high school in Jaruplund in South Schleswig. And finally I spent two periods at the Academy of Art in Odense. I was able to obtain grants for all of this. As I had no means of my own, I couldn't simply say that now I was going to be a painter and then buy everything I needed. But in the schools of art I was able to get to know the materials, to hold them in my hands and to acquaint myself with the various techniques. The schools of art were also important to me in that through them I made contact with others with the same interest as myself, some of whom were older and more experienced. It was a happy time for me even though I all the time worried about what was going on at home and of course went there every weekend. And that was necessary. I had to clear up the situation after the battle my parents had had with each other during the week. But I had the other days in the week for myself. Days when I could devote myself to what meant most for me.

One day while I was at the art high school in Holbæk, our neighbour at home rang to me to say that my mother had gone off the rails again. I must come home. Inspired by *The Works of Love*, which I read in the train on the way, I suddenly with complete clarity realised something that also applied to me, that is to say that Christ is the necessary link for those who want to meet God. Christ comes to you if you really want faith. Deep down in myself I have kept the memory of moments when I have felt a union with faith. Everything adds up in such moments. I am at one with creation. Whether alive or dead, I am with God. I had thereby escaped all fear, totally present in the face of God. With that conviction, you become a harmonious being who does not spend all your time thinking of satisfying your own needs, but of opening up to your neighbour. The neighbour you meet everywhere.

What I do is *my* responsibility. And what my mother did was *hers*. The responsibility that was mine on this day was to receive her with love. "Though shalt love thy neighbour" – that is the really difficult challenge. But at the same time, the demand that we should love our neighbour gives one great peace. Morals are something you must have in relation to yourself. You can't tell others how to act. We are all alone in the face of God. And we must not judge others. That is not our task. We must judge ourselves alone. A crucial change takes place in our lives when we realise that that is how things are.

I was not going to feel sorry for myself. Not the least bit! No, I was to help my neighbour. I was to be the Good Samaritan. Not to feel I was good. But because I was being called. And the person calling me was my mother. Irrespective of how dreadful she could be, she was in a situation in which, as the one closest to her, I had to help her. I used to grumble at her a great deal. Now I realised that what was needed was love. However, she became angry when I tried to help her. She wanted to go on drinking and taking all those pills on which she had become so dependent. But she finally accepted my love. She accepted it for the last four or five years of her life. As a result of all those years of abuse, she had destroyed her immune system. She suffered from arthritis and finally was consigned to a wheelchair until she died in 2002. I also managed to become reconciled with my father, who died in 1988.

Forgiveness for me came through Christianity. And it is a choice of an either-or. I couldn't call myself a Christian if I didn't forgive totally.

4.

My husband, Peter Brandes, and I live in Paris and Dublin, and we have a weekend cottage in Denmark 15 kilometres from the place where I lived as a child. But it's on the same stretch of coast. I couldn't imagine living close to my childhood home permanently, but would rather come and visit it and then go off again. I would like to retain that place as something secret, strange and unapproachable.

Occasionally I go there together with my sisters, and then we relive it all together. We remember every tree, every bush, all the flowers, we remember where we used to hide and jump out on each other. The beauty there is about it all means a great deal to me. The beauty that memory helps to create. If I settled near this place, I wouldn't experience it in the same way. Revisiting the places where my sisters and I were together so much and seeing the area is deeply moving. It is a treasure I refuse to relinquish. Nowhere else in the world contains such powerful personal experiences for me. But in no way do I deny all those dreadful things. No, they are part of it all. Returning to the landscape I knew as a child is a kind of reconciliation.

It also happens that I go along the road I followed in my childhood, which was also my road to school, and I remember it as being incredibly long. When I see it again today, it is so short that I am almost scared by it, as I also am on seeing the fruit trees in our little garden again, the trees we climbed and swung in. They almost look as though they have shrunk. The only thing that doesn't look smaller is the sea. Its vastness is the same. And the rock on which, as a child, I saw a white-tailed eagle is still there.

That day marked an epoch in my life. Dusk was falling, and I went down to the shore, eight or nine years old. I had a shock when I saw a white-tailed eagle on the rock a couple of metres out in the water. Never had I seen such a big bird – indeed I had no idea that such big birds even existed. What was I to do? Stay there or go away again? Whatever I did, I knew that the sight of this bird would go with me. I often picture it. The image is of the big bird's dark silhouette against the evening sky, while the waves are lapping at the shore.

Fundamentally, it was fascination with what you can't see, but which you can feel. Something really unknown – like, if I am to use a grand word, something divine in nature In nature, I felt that everything was being given to me and conversely, nothing demanded of me. It was a fantastic feeling – simply to receive.

5.

To me, working as an artist is a Christian and existential matter. And its external success – or possible lack of success –says nothing about the degree of compulsion. I create what I *must* create.

I made my first work as a church artist in 1996, in Øster Tørslev Church between Randers and Hadsund. The embellishment is a painting, a work already in existence, which is based on the story in Exodus of how God revealed Himself to Moses in the "guise" of a burning bush. What to me is the crucial point – that God reveals Himself without showing His face – can be seen again in a series of paintings from 1999 based on the account in Genesis of Jacob wrestling with the angel. Neither in these paintings do I portray God directly. The two figures wrestling are represented by two wings and a hip socket. The struggle certainly led to Jacob's being blessed, as he demanded, but he was also marked: A blow on his hip made him lame. Redemptive fulfilment also bears pain within it.

Any insight you gain entails pain. You have to go through the struggle, and if you can cope with it in a purely physical sense, also without subsequently pitying yourself, you are strengthened and at the same time grateful for the struggle, which has revealed you to yourself and cleansed you. That is why I perhaps quite instinctively chose Jacob wrestling with the angel as a motif.

I read the Old Testament again and again, and the images come to me while I am doing so. The biblical descriptions of nature are so fabulous and so dramatic – to me quite crucial as a foundation for Christianity. I do not consciously introduce myself into my images, but I start out from a universal truth: You must be prepared to live through whatever is your lot.

Those who from the beginning have emphasised the success I have had were simply not aware that behind it lay a kind of Jacobean struggle. I refused to tell anyone about it while my mother was alive. I didn't want to hurt her. I couldn't bring myself to let her see in writing what she and I had spoken of in confidence and in fact agreed on. It is one thing for a mother and daughter to talk to each other. It is something quite

JACOB WRESTLING
WITH THE ANGEL
Acrylic on canvas, 1998, 190 x 250 cm
Property of Deloitte, Copenhagen

54

different if you read that your daughter has told others about it. I knew that if I were to tell the story of my childhood, it would not have to be for my own sake, not as a therapy. I imagined that I could perhaps help others who had experienced something similar, that I could try to pass on my experiences to them and through my example show that it *is* possible to get through that kind of thing and achieve a harmonious life. In this way it would have a meaning. In reality I felt that it was almost an obligation on me to tell my story. I don't myself feel a need to "rummage around" in my own life, in all those things that my parents exposed my younger sisters and myself to in our childhood, but I would like to tell about it all if in this way I can be of help to others.

So I have done work with children that have been exposed to violence. The most important thing is to make it clear to these children that they must not become stuck in self-pity, that at some time or other they must forgive. Otherwise they will never get any further. I am glad if I can help someone for whom life has been and perhaps still is a nightmare to realise that there in fact is a possibility of escaping from the nightmare.

I don't think that it was because I had what in many respects was a terrible childhood that I became the person I am. Nor have I ever felt sorry for myself or worried about how I was to manage. And I have never felt a need to seek psychological help. What has helped me was and remains my close relationship to Christianity. At the same time the situation was that as long as I remained silent about all those things to which my sisters and I were exposed in those days, I often thought about it all only in fragmentary form. So when I seriously started talking about my childhood, things poured out and one memory led to the other. Sometimes I have also been asked about something that I hadn't actually noticed, and then after this I thought some thoughts through that I would otherwise never have thought through.

In this way, I have achieved a relationship with my childhood that is more serene than it was before I started talking about it. It's the positive aspect that interests me. The fact that I have come through if it with my head held high. On the other hand, I don't think that the violence implied in some of my paintings directly reflects my experiences as a child. It might be that there is sometimes a certain violent element reflected in my paintings, but this is not because I feel a need to express anger. I have no need at all to express anger. I have never thought in that way. When I turn to my paintings I forget all about myself. And I can't relate the fact of a violent childhood to them. What my sisters and I went through I think of mainly in relation to Christianity and forgiveness. Not in relation to my paintings. They belong after all to a quite different world.

I paint purely instinctively and have no need in my paintings to tell about a terrible childhood. The paint-

ROAD THROUGH LANDSCAPE
Acrylic on canvas, 2000, 260 x 360 cm
Property of Statens Museum for Kunst

ings are not private in this way. Personal perhaps, but not private. The nightmare was there, and it is a matter of looking that in the eyes, accepting and forgiving. The betrayal that my sisters and I experienced was clearly our lot. Now that is past. And so there I stand, freed, pristine again like a sheet of white paper, ready to receive. Nor is what fills my thoughts today either the nightmare or self-pity, but gratitude for having come out on the other side.

When, during my work, I abandon myself completely to a painting and it really takes over, I have no thoughts at all. I don't think of my childhood or my parents or of fear and trembling or anything else at all. It is solely the painting that is reality for me. And I paint entirely on its premises. It is as though there are pictures in the future waiting for me to paint them. Images that gradually come to me. During the process of creation I have no sense of what is going on; I know nothing. I am engrossed in the individual painting as though I myself am the motif in it. Afterwards, I can't really say anything about the finished work because it is part of something else that I can't explain. This total presence that I have in my paintings will, I feel, become increasingly purified as the years pass.

Christianity, the awareness of belonging to God, is what means most in my life. It's a matter of receiving life as a gift from God. And accepting it whether good or bad. But I cannot myself know what is good for me. And so I have neither special expectations nor desires in relation to my life. Apart from the fact that I would like to behave in a decent way. It is a great step to take – not to have a specific dream of what happiness is. But you can't know what happiness is for you. Only God knows that. There are many people who are dissatisfied and don't think that what they are doing is sufficiently exciting. They imagine that if only they could turn to something different, everything would be far better. But that is not how things are. An important condition for being happy is that you follow the road that is yours. Then possibilities will open up. And you must be open to them.

6.

When I paint, it is because the pictures demand to be painted. I am simply available. But first I have to find my way in to them. And dig them out. That is how I feel it. My first attempts, many, many of them, are of no interest whatever. The image only comes when I am calm. After that I break everything down that I have built up, perhaps except for a few fragments, but that is really nothing. Now it is the picture that decides. Reaching that stage is a fantastic experience. It is suddenly as it has to be. And what happens is each time equally

THE SECOND DAY
Acrylic on canvas, 2007, 250 x 210 cm
Private Collection, New York

inexplicable. Nothing I do with the conscious part of myself will help me to get there. It isn't like having a problem that I think can be solved in this way or that, after which I do it. In this situation I can simply not use my intellect, but I have to take a step further, a step out into some unknown territory where I myself am no longer present, and where I dare to open myself to receive something else.

I have never managed to go straight to a painting; I have never painted a picture harmoniously from start to finish. I have to go through this despair, this vast gloom, when nothing goes right. On the other hand I think I would be nervous if a painting came out right straight away. I would be distrustful of it. It is hard to go around in your studio every day, hard to experience your weakness. I become really upset when I have to go through these depressions. It is difficult to do anything else when, day after day in succession, you have a painting standing there crying out and screaming, but also sticking out its tongue at you. But I *do* go into my studio every day, simply so as not to become afraid of it. Even so, I *do* become afraid – of the lofty demands I make on myself and which I want to make on myself. And every day I think: What if I suddenly can't paint any more? You never know. For I am not in control of the paintings. It's the paintings that have control over me. This is a crucial distinction.

The actual creative process is a wearing one that takes many days. And it is difficult to concentrate on other tasks when you have a picture standing there that seems impossible to paint. But suddenly, one day, something happens. This inexplicable thing that I touched on before. There is no knowing when the great change will come. And there is nothing you can do to *make* it come.

There is nothing more demanding than to be creative. You become touchy and nervous. All your complexes about what you *can't* do well up in you. All the time. Living together with another artist means a great deal in this context. My husband and I both know exactly what is involved when the other is in the process of creating something. It produces a sense of solidarity. A place for tolerance when confronting an unreasonable situation.

We can talk completely openly about our work. I can't see my paintings from the outside because I am part of them. But Peter can see them from outside. As can I with his. And sometimes, when one of us can't get any further with our work, we can, indirectly and with a few small words, help the other to get going again. Peter might perhaps draw my attention to a specific part of a painting and compare the light in it with the light in a painting by Johan Thomas Lundbye. A comment of this kind can resolve a problem and help me on in my attempt to find the image I have briefly glimpsed. When I finally recognise it on the canvas, the painting is finished.

As I had from the start taken themes and derived inspiration from Christianity, the possibility of having my works integrated into a church context was a thought I had long secretly cherished. The union that the Church originally had with the people, a union of which our churches with their architecture and embellishments are still a living example, was broken when art was privatised and galleries and private financial interests came to assume a prominent role. But church art can in many ways be the ideal dialogue between the sacred, people's desire for a non-material contact and devotion to Christianity. So my joy was very great indeed when for the first time I was invited to undertake the embellishment of a church.

The preliminaries to an embellishment are not necessarily merely preliminaries, but can also be something in themselves. Anticipation. A sense of community. A meeting with the parish council that after getting to know my work more closely wanted me, just me, to give their church a new and distinctive character. At the first meetings with the parish council, the mood generally is – or generally becomes – positive and open. We are together on our way to taking a decision that will affect the life of the church and the congregation for years to come.

As a result of church embellishments, I have had amazing and moving discussions on faith and Christianity with people whom I would otherwise never have met. These people can sometimes ask me questions that are so unexpected that they open new perspectives to me of which I have not been aware. I think the fact that I am not a theologian plays some part here. It makes conversation easier. As an artist, you have a different view of many things in the church, and that is a good starting point for a dialogue. Especially when people realise the extent to which Christianity is part of my own life. I can go round a church with someone and for instance discuss with them how the light falls in the nave or talk about the history of this church. I can also reflect with them how important the task is on which they have decided – the task of undertaking a new embellishment. My experience then is that the sense that the embellishment of a church is a common undertaking is intensified as work proceeds. That it is a process that strengthens a parish's awareness of the value of the local church.

When I meet a parish council for the first time, its members sit there at first like stone statues. And I have certain odds against me: I live in France, not in Denmark, and I am a female artist. I can easily read the reservations in the looks they give me. But I have nothing to hide; I speak quite openly to them and they can ask about anything at all. This openness means that the mood gradually becomes more positive. And sometimes, when I am alone with people, it can lead to these amazing discussions and moving confessions on the part of people whose confidence means a great deal to me.

As time has gone on, I have worked with a great number of parish councils. It is my experience that they really consider things carefully when they are about to choose an artist. And art *does* these days play an important part with regard to a church. As I say, an embellishment provides a greater sense of community. A sense of warmth. And a delight in the church and the space within it. I have experienced this as something very positive. To talk of a spiritual revival is perhaps rather grandiloquent, but I receive letters from people who believe that the embellishments I have made have in fact meant a kind of spiritual revival for them. But it is a spiritual revival that is linked to the Word. It is important to emphasise that the painting is not there on its own. The priest might refer to it in his sermon. And then something can happen in the image.

Interest in the church must not only be an interest in a new altarpiece or a new kind of embellishment. People should come to the church to hear the Word. They must come to it as the sacred place it is. And I feel that as an artist I can tell people something about what kind of a place it is and also help to reveal it to them. I am convinced that art is of great importance in that context.

I do not undertake the embellishment of churches because I have had a special training in this. I have not. But I am endowed with a special passion as an artist. And as faith is the very focal point for me – because Christianity simply means everything to me – I feel that I can allow myself to work with the figure of Christ, as in fact I do. I can't produce theological exegeses from a pulpit, but I am completely on a level with the people who simply come to church. Meanwhile, with my paintings and in harmony with the sermon delivered by the priest, I can perhaps approach Christianity in a way that is neither didactic nor suggestive of superior knowledge. If they wish, people can seek to empathise with the paintings. People who are perhaps experiencing some great sorrow or some great joy. The paintings can help to tell them and everyone else present in the church that God is always here. For it is never God who deserts us, but always we who desert Him.

I can't distinguish between being a human being and being an artist. I don't live in one manner when I am in my studio and in general in my own world with art at its centre and then in a different manner when I am away from it all. I am always the same, the same seeker. When people ask me about something I answer as openly as I can. And I do that because I myself am a seeker. I have nothing specific in mind. In reality, I know nothing at all. I am simply someone who has to pass something on: whatever comes to me in the paintings.

When I am about to start on an embellishment, I am keen to listen as much as possible. At the same time I have to be completely free from personal problems and my own thoughts. I must listen for something else, something outside me, and open myself to it. I don't wonder what I am going to do here. I enter a church

CHRIST
Sketches for Skannerup Church
Acrylic on canvas, 2005, 55 x 42 cm
Private Collection

with a mind that is completely receptive and blank. Before this, I have looked at the landscape or the local town area that I have driven through to reach the church. And its surroundings form part of my starting point. Its position in an urban area or out in the country, on a hilltop or on flat agricultural land, by a marsh or a heath form part of my ballast when I am sitting in the church. The surroundings from which people have come over time when they have visited the church have affected the feel of it. So every single church is unique to me.

It happens frequently and in many churches that things enter the picture without anyone having thought of whether they really ought to be there. This might for instance be a candlestick or some chairs that don't really serve any purpose. They have simply been put there, and people have grown so accustomed to their presence that no one thinks of moving them. In this way a feeling of pettiness can have made its way into the church. But it is not intended to look like a living room. When I sit alone in the church and see everything with "fresh eyes", I notice things of this sort that don't belong there. In my imagination I clear the space and almost feel as though I am sitting at a computer and removing the things that are blocking it, spoiling the overall impression and distracting attention from what is essential. I do this taking into account the size of the church so that it can once again be associated with a holy space. In former times people would stand during mass in many mediaeval churches. The pews were later additions. The same applies to the panels that were put there to keep out damp and cold. But these panels are no longer necessary now that the churches are heated. They give a feeling of heaviness that ought not to be there, and it is a relief to be able to get rid of them. That kind of thing helps to introduce a feeling of lightness in the church.

As an artist coming from outside the parish I can point out the beauty in the church that people have perhaps never noticed or which they have perhaps over time lost a sense of, just as I can point out how this beauty can better come to its right. If you can really open people's eyes, you also open their hearts. And conversely: If you can speak to people's hearts out of your own heart, you also open their eyes.

In every embellishment that I have agreed to undertake, I have, when I have managed to fight my way out of all my own thoughts, suddenly seen what it is that the church in question wants me to do in this place. I see the totality, not in detail of course, for instance not the colours, but I see the most important thing, the *motif*. I then try to work my way towards what I have seen, towards what I feel is something that has been inspired in me. It is like a kind of revelation to me. It has nothing at all to do with me myself. For the experience doesn't come until I have become completely emptied, listening to the body of the church and the possibilities it presents. It is the church that determines what I am to do.

The nave, Raklev Church
Recently renovated with colouring
and simplification

64

When I have received what has been given to me, it has to form part of a concrete cohesive structure. I take into account the body of the church, this body in this church. What it says to me when I open myself to it is the only thing to which I pay attention. I don't wonder how little or how much knowledge of Christianity the people who will come into the church have. I sense the path I am to tread and then I follow it without knowing where that path is going to lead me.

The first time I meet the parish council I say nothing about what my thoughts are regarding the church or the embellishment I am perhaps to make. But when I have envisioned how the embellishment is to be, then that is how it *must* be. It's as simple as that. I back up one hundred per cent for the sketches that I subsequently summit. And if the parish council doesn't want me to carry out the task in the way I am suggesting, then I am not the right artist, and they must find another. I am prepared to discuss small practical changes, but the overriding artistic solution must stay. I do not submit alternative proposals.

When I am to meet a parish council after they have received my preparatory sketches, it is I who am making an offer. If they don't want to accept it, I simply go again. It doesn't bother me. I emphasise to the members of the parish council that they should take their time deciding on my proposal, and that they should do so without me myself being present. Then they can say what they think. If some members can't go along with the proposal, then it should be turned down. I want their full backing to go on. Otherwise nothing good will come of it. There might even be conflict between those who like my proposals and those who don't. I simply refuse to get mixed up in that sort of thing. I make no effort to convince such members of the council who may be in doubt. I present the proposal in all honesty, as I have envisioned it. There is no more to be said about that.

8.

As a child I was afraid. Also of God. Most of all because I couldn't see Him. When there were terrible gales or thunderstorms I thought it was God who was angry. But when I met Christianity, my fears vanished. Fundamentally, this is the actual change that has taken place in me as an adult. During my childhood, the Old Testament was present in nature, which is described so beautifully, and as the background to many of the events recounted, including the dreadful ones. In the New Testament, on the other hand, it is Christ who is central. We are given a figure. A face. In the Old Testament we only have the invisible God in nature – in the light, in a cloud, in a burning bush or in the ocean. With Christianity God walks into nature.

Stained glass
Raklev Church

I simply cannot occupy myself with the New Testament without also occupying myself with the Old Testament. The invisible God we know from that is made visible in Christ who time after time refers to the God of our fathers and to the Law of Moses. There is no denying the origins. And the origins are the God who condemns and punishes combined with the anticipation of the Messiah who is to come. For me there is complete cohesion between the Old and the New Testaments. As there is between the Crucifixion and Easter Morning.

When I am working with the Old Testament, I use a motif from it in the altar carpet, whereas the motif in the altarpiece is always from the New Testament. I can now, after it all, see how things have turned out. And this is because this is how the embellishment appears when I see it for the first time, when, indeed, it is revealed to me. I don't decide for myself; I don't think that now I had better have an Old Testament motif.

But I think the way it has worked out has the right effect: The members of the congregation who have chosen to receive Holy Communion bow their heads and in their absorption, on receiving the bread and the wine, they look down on the unseen God of the Old Testament, then the next moment when they look up again, they encounter Christ directly, face to face. In all the churches where I have been responsible both for the altar carpet and for the altarpiece, I have in a way given the Old Testament a basic role. That is to say that when you enter the church you see the figure of Christ approaching you, and when you bow your head before the altar you encounter the Old Testament as it really is: as the very foundation.

For instance, when I portray Jacob wrestling with the angel in an altarpiece, I do it not only so as to depict the struggle between the two. And I never do it as a clear image of this struggle, not as a complete and finished image. The content is not given to the viewer without further ado. We have ourselves to take part in the struggle. Of course the painting lives its own life, but is also lives by virtue of the viewer. If someone without a close relationship with Christianity sees one of my altarpieces, that person will perhaps believe they can see something other than Christ. Only if you look at the painting through the eyes of faith is it Christ you see.

At the same time, I have experienced my paintings awakening an interest in Christianity. There are people who have said to me that they didn't expect they would ever again bother about Christianity. But they say that my paintings have made them want to go back to the Bible. During the spring after 11 September 2001, when the Americans really were hurt, I had a large exhibition in New York. Three people came to me and told me in confidence that after that day they had lost all their faith, all their trust, and that they had simply refused to think of the Old or the New Testaments. Nevertheless, they had found their attention focused on one specific painting, the motif of which is the second day of Creation. They felt particularly drawn by

JACOB WRESTLING
WITH THE ANGEL
Acrylic on canvas, 1998, 97 x 80 cm
Private Collection

this painting. There was something about the light, something about grandeur. And they said they would go home and read the story of the Creation in the Bible, and they thanked me for through my painting inspiring them to do that.

According to Kierkegaard, the opposite of sin is not virtue, but faith. And for me the greatest sin to be found anywhere is to persuade people to doubt. It is so easy to persuade people to that. Doubt is the most present thing of all; indeed it is so easy to say to unhappy people that with all the dreadful things that are happening in the world it cannot possibly be true that God exists. But if you have faith in God, you can't lose that confidence. Even if you are in extreme distress, if you are shut up in a tiny space, or if you lose your arms and legs. If you have faith in your heart, this is the most essential thing you possess. And no one will ever be able to take it from you.

9.

As a church artist, you are naturally part of a tradition. Many people in Denmark have tried to identify my sources of inspiration and suggested Sven Havsteen-Mikkelsen and Niels Larsen Stevns among others. When I see the light in a painting by Stevns well, it's difficult to explain, but for me he is working with a Christian light. But although I am very fond of Stevns as an artist, I don't have him as an actual model. In general, I don't bother myself much with artists from or close to our own time. I won't risk being unconsciously influenced by them, but I try instead to open myself to the images that it has become my lot to paint.

So I prefer to go further back – to older artists whose manner of painting is very different from my own, but who provide me with great experiences. One example is Lundbye, who has always meant a great deal to me, but L.A. Ring has also been an influence on me. He was an atheist and certainly no church artist, but even so he says something to me, partly on account of the light in his paintings. The way in which he allows it to be reflected in the still waters in Roskilde Fjord is for me really a picture of eternity – though Ring himself probably didn't think of it in this way. When I see the sky reflected in Ring, I think that it can only be because the water is so motionless and radiant. If there had been only a slight motion in the water, the sky couldn't have been reflected. I go on from this to think that if faith is to be able to be reflected in a person, that person must also be calm.

Ring's works are possessed of an honesty and an unspoiled way of reflecting the light in landscapes that appear so chaste. He has made his mark on my view of the purity the light in Denmark can have at times. His

The Lily of the Field and
the Bird under the Sky
Monotype for a Søren Kierkegaard text
2009, 42 x 31 cm
Private Collection

70

paintings have so much to say to me and can actually produce a sense of recognition in me: "This is just like a painting by Ring". He had a great love of nature. No one can paint a quite ordinary bumpy unmade road as he can. He is able to turn it into a thing of infinite beauty. If he had not taught us really to *see* a road like this, we would say, "What a muddy mess!" But he brings out all the shades of brown and grey and like Lundbye has been a great eye-opener for me.

The fact that Ring was not a believer, however, does not mean that he would not be able to create church art. To my mind, that must be up to the individual artist. In my case, the paintings are a natural extension of my Christianity. Precisely because Christianity is the turning point in my life it is a great happiness to me that I have been allowed to embellish churches. But I will not set myself up as a judge of other artists. If a picture has been honestly painted, it must also be a valid painting. At the same time I must add that when I see a landscape done by an artist such as, for instance, Olaf Rude, I don't have the same feeling of its being a Christian landscape as I have every time I see a landscape by Larsen Stevns. It's clear there must be a difference. But again: I won't set myself up as a judge. And in addition, it is something to which it is difficult to relate and not least difficult to explain more precisely. Declaring oneself to be a Christian is in my view a significant step that results in great responsibility towards oneself and one's honesty. But the line taken is up to each separate individual. You are alone in it.

In that vibrant building that is a church, art is not permanent. Of course, I can feel that myself. In 100 years there will perhaps be other paintings where mine now hang. The attitude towards an artist can change, and that is how things are. But at the same time I think that it is difficult to define a concrete work and not declare it to be good or the opposite. Works on which I used not to be keen can now have a quite different effect on me. We can take Vilhelm Hammershøi as an example. He was terribly looked down on 50 years ago. People simply didn't understand the beauty in his paintings. The attitude towards him has changed remarkably. Or take L.A. Ring, whose paintings for me produce associations with both the Old and the New Testaments. In this respect, L.A. Ring perhaps worked quite unconsciously. He was at least unable to introduce his atheism into his work. Or perhaps he was unable to introduce it in the way he perhaps wanted. The conclusion must be that even a declared atheist can paint works that move one profoundly in relation to Christianity. Artists seem not to be able to decide that for themselves.

10.

Of course it is wonderful to be allowed to work in churches. I am grateful for the commissions. But it is just as natural for me to paint a picture for a church as to paint one that is *not* for a church. Whatever the context in which I paint a picture, I feel that I am doing what I must. And I never think of it in relation to anything or anyone. Doing what I must gives me a profound sense of peace.

At the same time, my feeling is that I would not be able to paint Christ if it were not intended for a church. To me, a painting of Christ belongs to the embellishment of a church. I will not paint a figure of Christ simply in order to paint this motif. It must have a higher meaning.

When I produce a painting for a church, I am very careful not to feel any self-satisfaction. "Pride" is one of the worst words I know. I can't stand it when someone asks me if I am not proud of having completed a work of embellishment. I am not proud, but humble. For of course it is not by virtue of myself that I create the paintings. I have had a task, which is now completed. And that is that. And with that I leave the stage. After completing a task, I continue my life as a Christian. I don't wallow in my own things and I don't go around looking at what I have done. When this happens on occasion, I feel myself to be a guest on a visit. All visits can give delight or the opposite. But the works are still there.

THE ARTIST'S THOUGHTS ON THE CHURCH EMBELLISHMENTS

ØSTER TØRSLEV CHURCH

Painting on the south side of the nave.
Embellishment consecrated in 1996

Text inspiring the embellishment
Motif for the painting: "The burning bush", Exodus 3, 2-6

EMBELLISHMENT OF ØSTER TØRSLEV CHURCH

I had my first exhibition in a disused church, St Nicholas' Church, in Copenhagen. This was something of a paradox for me as from the very start I had taken Christianity as the source of my themes and inspiration. The union that art had originally represented between the people and a spiritual experience was broken when art was privatised and financial interests came to play an ever increasing role.

Church art could in many ways be the ideal dialogue between the sacred and people's desires and dreams of an immaterial contact with experiences that can lead to devotion to, for instance, Christianity.

The New Carlsberg Foundation bought one of my paintings with a motif inspired by the Old Testament account of Moses' meeting with the invisible God in the form the of the burning bush (Exodus 3, 2-6):

"And the angel of the Lord appeared unto him in a flame of fire out of the midst of a bush; and he looked, and, behold, the bush burned with fire, and the bush was not consumed. And Moses said, I will now turn aside, and see this great sight, why the bush is not burnt. And when the Lord saw that he turned aside to see, God called unto him out of the midst of the bush and said, Moses, Moses. And he said, Here am I. And he said, Draw not nigh hither: put off thy shoes from off thy feet, for the place whereon thou standest is holy ground. Moreover he said, I am the God of thy father, the God of Abraham, the God of Isaac, and the God of Jacob. And Moses hid his face; for he was afraid to look upon God."

The painting was hung in Øster Tørslev Church near Randers and was the beginning for me of my work with church art.

THE BURNING BUSH
Acrylic on canvas, 1995, 300 x 200 cm

77

SKELUND CHURCH

Painting placed in a freshly gilded altarpiece frame. Acrylic on canvas.
Altar carpet woven in wool, cotton, flax and silk.
Weavers Frédérique Bachellerie and Peter Schönwald, Atelier 3, Paris.
Two chasubles. Kashmir, velour, silk and gold and silk embroidery,
Tailors Susse Thorseng and Kristina Funder Buch.
Embellishment consecrated in 1999. Architect Poul Brøgger. Gilder Ove Olsen.

Texts inspiring the embellishment
Altarpiece motif: "Noli me tangere", John 20, 16-17
Motif on altar carpet: "Jacob wrestling with the angel", Genesis 32, 24-32.

EMBELLISHMENT OF SKELUND CHURCH

My first extensive church embellishment was in Skelund Church near Hadsund.

What was needed here was a new altarpiece and a new altar carpet in addition to deciding on colours for the body of the church. I have since made two chasubles for the same church, and two more are in preparation. In Skelund, I tried to portray Christ on Easter Morning, arisen and standing before the open grave (John 20, 11-18):

"But Mary stood without at the sepulchre weeping: and as she wept, she stooped down, and looked into the sepulchre, and seeth two angels in white sitting, the one at the head, and the other at the feet, where the body of Jesus had lain. And they say unto her, Woman, why weepest thou? She said unto them, Because they have taken away my Lord, and I know not where they have laid him. And when she had thus said, she turned herself back, and saw Jesus standing, and knew not that it was Jesus. Jesus saith unto her, Woman, why weepest thou? Whom seekest thou? She, supposing him to be the gardener, saith unto him, Sir, if thou have borne him hence, tell me where thou has laid him, and I will take him away. Jesus saith unto her, Mary. She turned herself and saith unto him, Rabboni, which is to say, Master. Jesus saith unto her, Touch me not; for I am not yet ascended to my Father: but go to my brethren, and say unto them, I ascend unto my Father, and your Father; and to my God and your God. Mary Magdalene came and told the disciples that she had seen the Lord, and that he had spoken these things unto her."

It was not a coincidence that I chose Christ arising on Easter Morning. It was necessary for me to portray this most important moment in Christianity as I certainly viewed this undertaking as my first church embellishment, but I did not know whether it might be the last. So I was keen to immerse myself in this essential motif.

NOLI ME TANGERE
Altarpiece before mounting
in altar frame

The altar carpet in front of the motive of the resurrection motif has as its motif Jacob wrestling with the angel (Genesis 32, 25-32):

"And when he saw that he prevailed not against him, he touched the hollow of his thigh; and the hollow of Jacob's thigh was out of joint as he wrestles with him. And he said, Let me go, for the day breaketh. And he said, I will not let thee go except thou bless me. And he said unto him, What is thy name? And he said, Jacob. And he said, Thy name shall be called no more Jacob, but Israel: for as a prince has thou power with God and with men, and hast prevailed. And Jacob asked him, and said, Tell me, I pray thee, thy name? And he said, Wherefore is it that thou does ask after my name? And he blessed him there. And Jacob called the same of the place Penuel: for I have seen God face to face, and my life is preserved. And as he passed over Penuel the sun rose upon him, and he halted upon his thigh.

The kneeling communicant looks at the invisible God in the altar carpet, but after the Eucharist receives the blessing of the risen Christ in the altarpiece.

JACOB WRESTLING WITH THE ANGEL
Altar carpet

Entrance area seen from the nave
Altarpiece and carpet

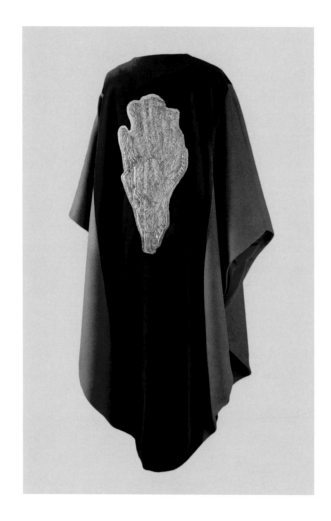

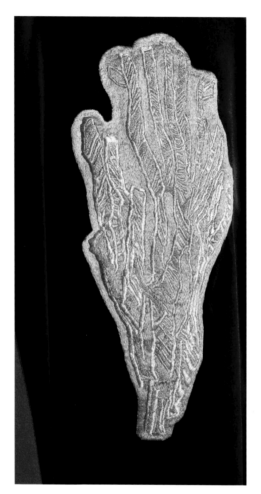

In addition to my embellishment of Skelund Church, I have been given the task of making a green and a white chasuble. On the back of the green chasuble the invisible God is present as the burning bush. On the front of it there is a tapestry representing three golden leaves as symbols of growth.

Skelund Church chasubles

 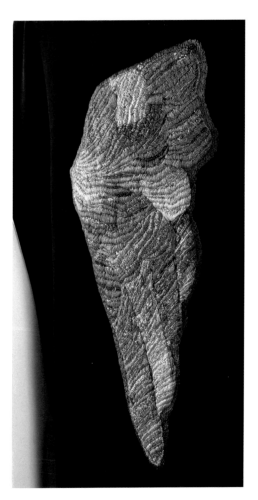 

On the back of the white chasuble the principal motif is a wing, referring to the dove of the Holy Spirit and Christ's baptism and presence. On the front of this chasuble there is an embroidered star announcing the birth of Christ. All the embroideries are made of a variety of gold and metal threads, so that the motifs keep light in themselves, but also radiate light.

GRINDERSLEV CHURCH

Two stained glass windows in the tower room. A painted sheet with motif fired in the glass,
a sheet of cut, mouth-blown glass.
Altar stone in a single piece of fired red clay.
Colour scheme for the entire church interior.
Embellishment consecrated in 2001. Architect Poul Brøgger, MAA. Tommerup Keramiske Værksted.
Glazier Per Steen Hebsgaard, Jannik Kvetny.

Texts inspiring the embellishment
Motif for the southern end of the tower room: "Ear of corn, crown of thorns and spring", "The Eucharistic bread
and wine and baptism".
Motif for the west window in the tower room: "The Road to Emmaus", Luke 24, 13-16.

EMBELLISHMENT OF GRINDERSLEV CHURCH

My art is borne of a visionary experience, a single starting point, and is in contrast to the alternative view of art, in which the understanding comes first and the vision afterwards.

My first impression of Grinderslev Church was the experience of a church that was very large for a village.

I took delight in the magnificent play of colours in the granite ashlars covered here and there with golden lichen and I admired the varied shades of red brick on the north wall in their interplay with the granite.

With its wonderful Romanesque apse and its many details, for instance the magnificent priest's entrance with the double rope ornament and its looped cross standing on a lion and a griffin, the architecture of this church is considered to be some of the finest Romanesque art in Denmark.

The experience inside was no less fascinating. My first impressions were quite overwhelming, and I was filled with delight and gratitude at being allowed to make my contribution to the long succession of traces of past times that are hidden or emerge in most of our churches.

I coloured all the woodwork, emphasising impressions from the greys of the granite and the golden shades of the lichen on it. The church inspired me to render a message of light. From the very first moment, I felt that the body of the church had about it something of the expression of the first Easter Morning. The extremely powerful bared altar lacked a top that could rival the bright colours in the Renaissance wall paintings and the altarpiece. Of course, this had to be a single piece of red clay, fired in Tommerup Teglværk, which is probably the first and only altar top of this kind in Denmark. In this way I also established a link to the beautiful red bricks on the north wall of the church.

Stained glass in the porch

86

Then I had the idea that a stained glass window to the west would create an essential balance. The parish council accepted this proposal. The tower room with its beamed ceiling has two deeply recessed windows in the Romanesque arched style – one facing south and one placed very centrally and facing west. The window to the south is hidden unless you enter the tower room. Facing south I have designed a stained glass window with a motif that starts out from the clerical door's beautiful looped, circle-enclosed cross. But also starting out from the quite unique granite cross standing free in the landscape a few kilometres east of the church. –

If you go from Grinderslev Church past the holy well that represented the basis of the wealth enjoyed by the monastery and church, a secret place where the water, the water of life and the water of baptism still flows, you discover standing in the flat landscape the beautiful, simple granite cross with a suggestion of cable ornamentation and ears of corn hidden in the weathered surface.

The bottom section of the stained glass window has this spring as its motif. Resting on the water of baptism, an ear of corn rises up and is transformed into a cross, and at the top there is a blood red crown of thorns. I have tried to combine the symbols of the Eucharist, the bread and the wine, with baptism and thus the congregation's entry into life.

The west window is seen in continuation of the aisle, and at the exit from the church people's eyes are naturally turned in that direction. As a motif for this I chose "The Road to Emmaus" (Luke 24, 13-16), where departure from the church thus continues with the hope and desire that people will meet the person the service is all about. I have been keen to create a road that is golden, again the power of light over darkness, a motif I have worked on in several paintings.

"And behold, two of them went that same day to a village called Emmaus, which was from Jerusalem about threescore furlongs. And they talked together of all these things which had happened. And it came to pass that, while they communed together and reasoned, Jesus himself drew near, and went with them. But their eyes were holden that they should not know him."

In this way, I have attempted to allow the light in the tower porch, which is now no longer daylight, but a spiritual light created by the remarkable way in which it filters in through the various pieces of glass, to be the congregation's final experience after service, on their way out, on their way home or elsewhere.

Stained glass in the porch

HOLSTED CHURCH

Altarpiece created as a glass mosaic. A painted sheet with motif burned in the glass, a sheet of cut, mouth-blown glass.
Granite altar top.
Bronze dish for the font.
Baptismal dish, baptismal jug, chalice, host box, paten all modelled and cast in bronze with enamels added to the baptismal dish. Chalice and cruet gilt inside.
Embellishment consecrated 2001. Architect: Sahls Tegnestue. Glaziers: Per Steen Hebsgaard, Jannik Kvetny.
Stucco workers Brdr. Funder. Bronze foundry: Fonderia Mariani at Pietra Santa.
Enamel work: Sidsel and Steffen Storm. Gilding and inserted silver: Per Sax Møller.

Texts inspiring the embellishment
Motif in the stained glass: "I am the way and the truth and the life", John 14, 6.
Baptismal dish and jug: "Wings".
Cruet: "Bunch of Grapes".
Chalice: "Crown of Thorns".
Paten and dish: "Ears of corn",
Candlesticks: "Burning Bush".

EMBELLISHMENT OF HOLSTED CHURCH

It is important to me to emphasise that church art becomes an extension of the presentation of the New Testament message and not a matter of a cultural art exhibition. I believe that the singing of hymns and the light in the churches and the liturgical ritual help to open the mind and the senses to the New Testament message in the same way as pictorial art can open the senses.

The very light in the churches emerges by virtue of the architecture and the traditionally constructed church with nave and chancel as more than everyday light in the symbolical body of the church. Stained glass windows originated from a desire to emphasise this dimension in the emanations of the church. The light, which is the symbol of Christ's presence, was there in a quite different way when filtered through coloured glass. This was the background to my huge 5 x 7 metre altarpiece for the new church at Holsted near Næstved. Here, the altarpiece constitutes a monumental glass window behind the altar, and in it I have tried to present Christ as the way, the truth and the life (John 14, 5-7):

I AM THE WAY AND
THE TRUTH AND THE LIFE
Stained glass altarpiece

"Thomas saith unto him, Lord, we know not whither thou goest; and how can we know the way? Jesus saith to him, I am the way, the truth, and the life: no man cometh unto the Father but by me. If ye had known me, ye should have known my Father also: and from henceforth ye shall know him, and have seen him."

God's very image, Christ, stands there featureless. He stands there intangible, as when God revealed Himself to Moses in the burning bush. On the other hand, the God of faith remains without facial features. Only in a flicker of colour or as a silhouette can the risen Christ just be discerned.

I AM THE WAY
AND THE TRUTH AND THE LIFE
Stained glass altarpiece,
before the installation of the altar rail

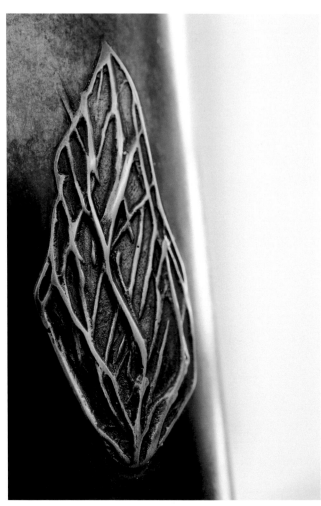

Altar candles, host box and paten
Patinated bronze

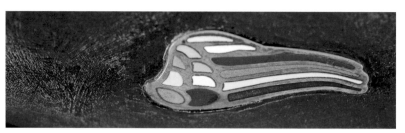

Details of baptismal jug, paten and baptismal dish
Baptismal dish
Patinated bronze and enamel

HYLLEHOLT CHURCH

Three paintings set in newly gilded altarpiece frame. Acrylic on canvas.
Altar carpet woven in wool, cotton, flax, silk and metal thread.
Two chasubles,
Altar cloth with embroidery in gold representing ears of corn.
Colouring of the entire church interior including capitals.
Embellishment consecrated in 2002. Architect: Jesper Herbert Nielsen, MAA, Arp og Nielsens Tegnestue.
Weavers: Frédérique Bachellerie and Peter Schönwald, Atelier 3, Paris.
Tailors: Susse Thorseng and Kristina Funder Buch.
Gilder: Ove Olsen.

Texts inspiring the embellishment
Altarpiece motif: "The Ascension", Acts 1, 9-11.
Altar carpet motif: "Moses wishing to see the glory of God", Exodus 33, 17-23.

EMBELLISHMENT OF HYLLEHOLT CHURCH

Hylleholt Church was built in the Neo-Gothic style at the end of the 19th century and can boast some fine details and solid building traditions. When I was given the task, the church lacked light and structure and did not open itself to one who wanted to understand the Gospel message. That is how I conceived the body of the church.

My embellishment encompassed a triptych altarpiece in the old frame, an altar carpet and a new colour scheme for the church in addition to a new altar cloth and two chasubles. A further two are in preparation.

The altarpiece shows the moment when Christ is together with and speaks to His disciples before leaving this earth (Acts 1, 7-12):

"It is not for you to know the times or the seasons, which the Father hath put in his own power. But ye shall receive power, after that the Holy Ghost is come upon you: and ye shall be witnesses unto me both in Jerusalem, and in all Judæa, and in Samaria, and unto the uttermost part of the earth. And when he had spoken these things, while they beheld, he was taken up: and a cloud received him out of their sight. And while they looked steadfastly toward heaven as he went up, behold, two men stood by them in white apparel; which also said, Ye men of Galilee, why stand ye gazing up into heaven? This same Jesus, which is taken up from you into heaven, shall so come in like manner as ye have seen him go into heaven.

THE ASCENSION
The altarpieces before mounting
in the altar frame

THE ASCENSION
The chancel and the body of the church

101

Before the altar, the altar carpet describes the moment when Moses stands in a cleft in the rock and sees God go by in all His glory (Exodus 3, 17-23):

"And the Lord said unto Moses, I will do this thing also that thou hast spoken: for thou hast found grace in my sight, and I know thee by name. And he said, I beseech thee, shew me thy glory. And he said, I will make all my goodness pass before thee, and I will proclaim the name of the Lord before thee; and will be gracious to whom I will be gracious, and will shew mercy on whom I will shew mercy. And he said, Thou canst not see my face: for there shall no man see me and live. And the Lord said, Behold there is a place by me, and thou shalt stand upon a rock: and it shall come to pass while my glory passeth by that I will put thee in a cleft of the rock and will cover thee with my hand while I pass by. And I will take away mine hand, and thou shalt see my back parts: but my face shall not be seen.

Once more, it is important to me that the communicant should first sense the presence of the invisible God via the altar carpet. After receiving Holy Communion communicants look up and in the altarpiece see the visible Christ.

MOSES BEHIND THE GLORY
OF THE LORD
Altar carpet

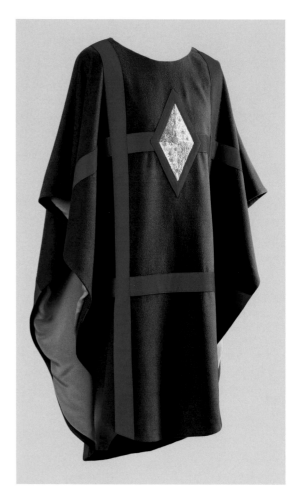

Chasubles are textile art, and fabric is characterised by the fact that it can be folded. I emphasise this and had it in mind when deciding on the material and the construction of the motif. The fabric is cashmere wool, which with its silk lining forms natural folds. This means that a shape and a motif emerge quite differently when the fabric is stretched out from when it hangs in folds. The green chasuble expresses growth with its colour. The green takes shape beneath the blue sky, which is recreated in the lining of the chasuble. The two side panels of the altarpiece also have these blues and greens as their predominant colours. And the small embroideries on the altar cloth are decorated with ears of corn and blue flower buds. Cornflowers. We find them again in the rhomboid front of the chasuble. Above the green chasuble's square embroidered landscape on the back a golden ear of corn can be seen floating. It has the bread and thus the Body of Christ hidden within it.

Hylleholt church chasubles

104

The idea behind the white chasuble with the stars in a rhomboid shape on the front is an attempt to herald the glad tidings that Christ's birth is. The Star of Bethlehem. This is underlined by the golden bands and the motif in the square on the back, where a golden star shines over a landscape. The symbol of light and ascension is hidden is the golden star

KULLERUP CHURCH

Two stained glass windows in the porch, a painted glass sheet with motif burned into the glass. A sheet of mouth-blown coloured cut glass.
Consecrated in 2002. Glaziers: Per Steen Hebsgaard, Jannik Kvetny.

Texts inspiring the embellishment
The motif in the stained glass on the east side of the porch: "The burning bush", Exodus 3, 2-6.
Motif on the west: "The Vine", John 15, 1-5.

EMBELLISHMENT OF KULLERUP CHURCH

The motif in the east window is the Burning Bush (Exodus 3, 2-6):

"And the angel of the Lord appeared unto him in a flame of fire out of the midst of a bush; and he looked, and, behold, the bush burned with fire, and the bush was not consumed. And Moses said, I will now turn aside, and see this great sight, why the bush is not burnt. And when the Lord saw that he turned aside to see, God called unto him out of the midst of the bush and said, Moses, Moses. And he said, Here am I. And he said, Draw not nigh hither: put off thy shoes from off thy feet, for the place whereon thou standest is holy ground. Moreover he said, I am the God of thy father, the God of Abraham, the God of Isaac, and the God of Jacob. And Moses hid his face; for he was afraid to look upon God."

A motif I have worked with before, but which I have always wanted to transfer to stained glass, as it is about light and the power of light through God. If anything can give an impression of this radiance, it is stained glass, and especially when it is turned to the east and imbibes the morning sunshine. I believe that the congregation coming to church in the morning will in this way both on arriving and departing from the church be confronted with the same possible miracle as Moses on the mountain. That at least is my hope.

The window facing west contains the motif from the New Testament centre on the true vine (John 15, 1-5):

"I am the true vine, and my Father is the husbandman. Every branch in me that beareth not fruit he taketh away: and every branch that beareth fruit, he purgeth it, that it may bring forth more fruit. Now ye are clean through the word which I have spoken unto you. Abide in me, and I in you. As the branch cannot bear fruit of itself, except it abide in the vine, no more can ye, except ye abide in me. I am the vine, ye are the branches…"

THE BURNING BUSH

It is important to me to link the New and the Old Testaments in this way, and where God's invisible presence is turned to the east it is important to introduce His Son's presence facing God's light.

As these windows are not particularly big, they require a couple of motifs that do not need much action, which it is difficult to portray over such a small area. For that reason, I have chosen a couple of symbolical motifs that almost have emblematic power within them.

The porch is also a place you go through, where you do not sit in contemplation as you do in the church, so what is required is rather a signal – a reminder, a statement, which in a simplified form tells of something essential.

THE TRUE VINE
The reflection of the true vine

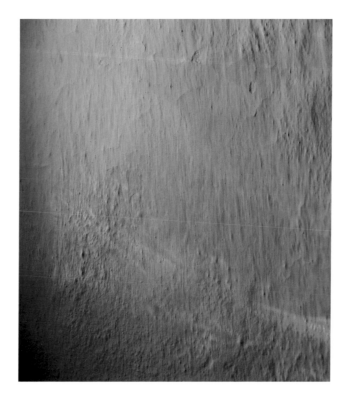 

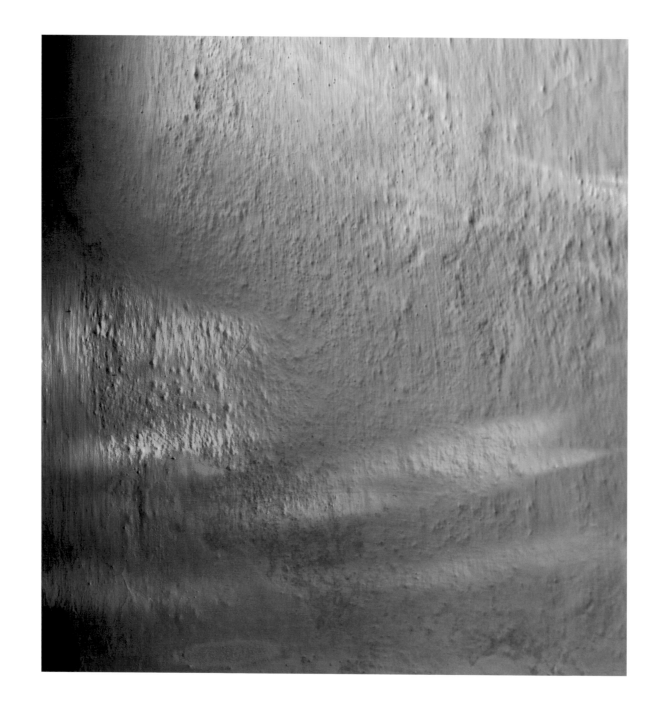

110

THE BURNING
BUSH
The reflection of the
true vine

111

FREDERIKS CHURCH

Painting set in a newly gilded altarpiece frame, acrylic on canvas.
Altar carpet woven in wool, cotton, flax, silk and metal thread.
Baptismal jug and baptismal dish, solid silver with relief added.
Colouring of the entire church interior.
The embellishment consecrated in 2003. Architect Thomas Meedom-Bæch, MAA. Gilder: Ove Olsen.
Weavers: Frédérique Bachellerie and Peter Schönwald, Atelier 3, Paris. Silversmith: Per Sax Møller.
The silver was consecrated in 2010 along with an original font refurbished by the artist, cleaned and gilded.

Texts inspiring the embellishment
Motif on the altarpiece: "The new covenant", Hebrews 9, 1-28.
Motif on the altar carpet: "The ark of the covenant" (Exodus 25, 1-40).
Baptismal dish and jug with the motif: "Wing".

EMBELLISHMENT OF FREDERIKS CHURCH

Frederiks Church is not a big one. Nor is it the oldest church in Denmark, but a church from the end of the 18th century built by Frederik V for a congregation of hard-working. Christian Germans who came to this area to cultivate a stubborn heath. They subsequently became known as the potato Germans.

When I entered this modest church for the first time, I was taken by its proportions and its simplicity.

I felt that this church was redolent of prayer, and the very harsh and impoverished conditions confronting the first people worshipping in the church were reflected in the church's restrained appearance. Extremely simple as an altarpiece can be in itself, a genuine faith hidden behind its message is an essential requirement.

When the parish council asked me to make a new altarpiece for the church, to gild its old frame, to create a new altar carpet in front of the altar and to bring colour to the body of the church, I was delighted to undertake the task. You can honour your faith with gifts to what cannot be measured.

The Old Testament contains an account of how the covenant was borne through the desert and across mountains, and when a halt was called, it was erected in a tent. In this tent there was a sacred place that was hidden from the people and which contained the covenant. This is described in part as follows (Exodus 25):

THE NEW COVENANT
THE ARK OF THE COVENANT
Part of the altar

"And the Lord spake unto Moses, saying, Speak unto the children of Israel, that they bring me an offering: of every man that giveth it willingly with his heart ye shall take my offering. And this is the offering which ye shall take of them: gold, and silver, and brass. And blue, and purple, and scarlet, and fine linen, and goats' hair." "And thou shalt put into the Ark the testimony which I shall give thee. And thou shalt make a mercy seat of pure gold: two cubits and a half shall be the length thereof, and a cubit and a half the breadth thereof. And thou shalt make two cherubims of gold, of beaten work shalt thou make them, in the two ends of the mercy seat." "And thou shalt make a candlestick of pure gold: of beaten work shall the candlestick be made: his shaft, and his branches, his bowls, his knops and his flower, shall be of the same."

The reverence for the holiest things and towards God, which is expressed in the rich gifts described is the motif I have tried to portray in the altar carpet.

When the communicants kneel before this carpet, which tells of such riches, it is to be hoped they will be filled with reverence towards the hidden God to whom these gifts are presented. And after the Eucharist I hope that their eyes will be directed up towards the altarpiece and the blessing following.

THE ARK OF THE COVENANT
Altar carpet

115

Here, I have portrayed the moment that is described in the New Testament in the Letter to the Hebrews Chapter 9. It is told that Christ has sacrificed Himself and is no longer the invisible God of the Old Testament, but now having given His own Blood to wipe away sin by His sacrifice, He emerges through the curtain and is the new covenant.

The invisible God, who hid behind the rich gifts of the altar carpet now steps visibly forward and comes to meet us in the golden frame of the altarpiece (Hebrews 9, 26-28):

"But now once in the end of the world hath he appeared to put away sin by the sacrifice of himself. And as it is appointed unto men once to die, but after this the judgement: So Christ was once offered to bear the sins of many; and unto them that look for him shall he appear the second time without sin unto salvation."

THE NEW COVENANT
Altarpiece prior to mounting
in the altar frame

117

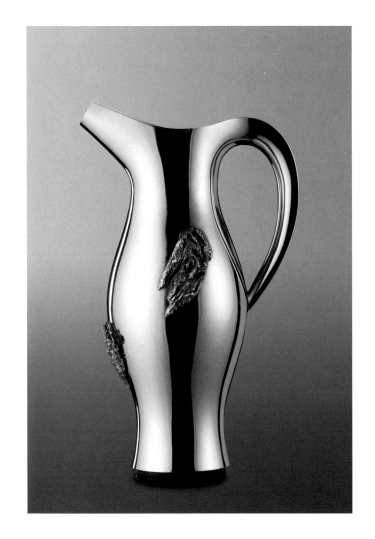 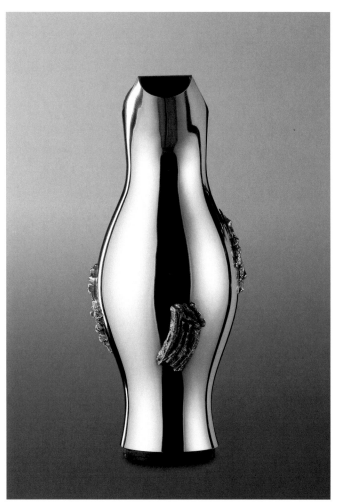

118

The Holy Spirit is revealed in Christ's face the moment John the Baptist baptises Him in the River Jordan. A bird, probably a dove, hovers above the act of baptism. I have used this symbol by modelling a bird's wing on the bottom of the baptismal dish and on the sides of the baptismal jug. I have fashioned the wing on the bottom of the dish in such a relief manner that when the water is poured into the dish, the wing is also transformed into ripples on the water's surface. This remarkable sight, the water, which is waves which in themselves are the wing's feathers, proclaims that inexplicable thing that the Holy Spirit represents. The bird's wings also become the wings with which the angel protects the little child. Dish and jug were created as hollowware in sterling silver by the master silversmith Per Sax Møller, without whose great sense of shape and technical ability it would not have been possible to complete this work.

The gilder Ove Olsen has used his skill to match the font to the gilding on the altar frame, which he had done previously.

Two stained glass windows in the north aisle. A sheet with motif burned into the glass, a sheet of cut, mouth-blown coloured glass.
The embellishment consecrated in 2004. Glaziers: Per Steen Hebsgaard, Jannik Kvetny.

Texts inspiring the embellishment
Motif in west window: "Christ", Matthew 17, 5.
Motif in north window: "Christ and Berenice", Mark 5, 25-35.

THE EMBELLISHMENT OF STOENSE CHURCH

My thoughts concerning the two stained glass windows in the aisle of Stoense Church start out from the fact that we are talking of one window facing north, which never receives any sunlight while that facing west catches the light late in the day when the light is fading.

So from a formal point of view I chose to make the north window graphically simple with a small number of colours, as is demanded by the weaker light. The north window is also the one seen at the greatest distance by parishioners when they stand in the central aisle and look towards it. The simple signs in the window will then emerge with the greatest force.

The west window must be endowed with more splendid colours and complexity, as it is experienced at a lesser distance, and especially the sun in the west will illuminate it beautifully and thus send its colours into the side aisle and illumine the wall opposite with colour.

The contents of the two windows are based on the following texts:
The west window (Matthew 17, 5):

"While he yet spake, behold, a bright cloud overshadowed them; and behold a voice out of the cloud, which said, "This is my beloved Son, in whom I am well pleased; hear ye him."

The essence of the stained glass window is both the present light, but also the intangible light that emerges when the window is lit from outside. In the text, the invisible God is present in the cloud – that is to say in the light; and with His words, God calls upon His Son, who appears. In this way, the message of the text is also united with the essence and character of the window. Where Christ is thus present in this window with the light behind, he can just be sensed in the subdued light of the north window. The starting point for the content of the north window is Mark 5, 25-35:

Stained glass
West window

120

121

122

"And a certain woman, which had an issue of blood twelve years, and had suffered many things of many physicians, and had spent all that she had, and was nothing bettered, but rather grew worse, when she had heard of Jesus, came in the press behind, and touched his garment. For she said, If I may touch but his clothes, I shall be whole. And straightway the fountain of her blood was dried up, and she felt in her body that she was healed of that plague. And Jesus, immediately knowing in himself that virtue had gone out of him, turned him about in the press, and said, Who touched my clothes? And his disciples said unto him, Thou seest the multitude thronging thee, and sayest thou, Who touched me? And he looked round about to see her that had done this thing. But the woman fearing and trembling, knowing what was done in her, came and fell down before him and told him all the truth. And he said unto her, Daughter, thy faith had made thee whole; go in peace, and be whole of thy plague."

The motif in the north window is that garment of Christ's from which the healing and saving power flows out. On the west window He is still visibly present, but on the north window an invisible power goes from Him to the woman, who is saved by her faith.

Stained glass
North window

124

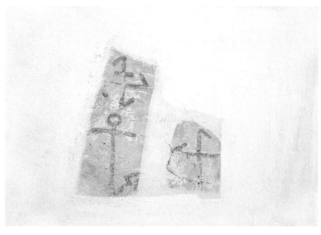

Stained glass
West and north windows
Details of the windows and elements in the church

125

SKANNERUP CHURCH

A painting on the end wall of the nave, which is seen on leaving. Acrylic on canvas,
Gilt frame with sheaf of corn in relief. Colouring of the entire interior of the church.
The embellishment was consecrated in 2005. Architect: Anders Kjærsgard, Årstiderne Arkitekter, Silkeborg.
Stucco workers: Brdre. Funder. Gilder: Ove Olsen.

Texts inspiring the embellishment
The motif in the painting: "Christ", Matthew 28, 18-20.

EMBELLISHMENT OF SKANNERUP CHURCH

My church embellishments have so far been concerned with motifs from the period in the New Testament relating to Christ's acts and Resurrection.

This is a clear choice on my part, in which I seek to emphasise with my paintings that after His resurrection, Christ became visible as a saviour, a bringer of good tidings, and a guiding star. It says, in Matthew 28, 18-20:

"And Jesus came and spake unto them, saying, 'All power is given unto me in heaven and in earth. Go ye therefore, and teach all nations, baptizing them in the name of the Father, and of the Son, and of the Holy Ghost. Teaching them to observe all things whatsoever I have commanded you: and, lo, I am with you alway, even unto the end of the world.'"

These words are important for Christians to carry with them, not least when they have attended divine service and are leaving the church. So much takes place in the church facing forward by the altar, but when we go out of the church and in doing so take leave of the building and the message contained in the ritual, it is my wish that my icon-like image on the west wall may be a greeting on departure, a good way of taking leave of what has just taken place.

The golden frame around the painting gathers the light and radiates light. The relief-like ears of corn tell us of the local harvests, but especially of the corn that becomes bread, and which again is the symbol of Christ's Body.

I have chosen colours for the wood in the church that are related to the light from the gold and the thought of the gift of corn. Given my colours, the heavy presence of the organ has achieved a lightness that accords with my entire wish to give the church light. The occasional touches of gilt contribute to this sense of lightness. As though in a print. My image for the departure seeks to give an impression of Christ's face. He will be present for those who believe.

Picture on leaving
Acrylic on canvas
Modelled gold frame
Nave p. 128-129

ST CATHERINE'S CHURCH – SCT. CATHARINÆ KIRKE

Altar carpet woven in wool, silk, cotton and flax.
Monumental painting on the south wall of the church. Acrylic on canvas.
Embellishment consecrated in 2005 and 2009.
Weavers: Frédérique Bachellerie and Peter Schönewald, Atelier 3, Paris.

Texts inspiring the embellishment
Motif in the altar carpet: "The Burning Bush", Exodus 3, 1-7.
Motif in the painting: The mediaeval ballad of Queen Dagmar.

EMBELLISHMENT OF ST CATHERINE'S CHURCH

My altar carpet in St. Catherine's Church in Ribe starts out from the view that the altarpiece in the church in all its multiplicity and its exploration of New Testament motifs, with the motif of the Last Supper at its centre, demands a carpet that stands out in its simplicity. But it should also have a content linked to the Old Testament as the foundation on which the New Testament is based.

The motif I chose is the Burning Bush. I have worked with this central motif many times and in materials as diverse as painting, cut glass and graphic art. This is the first time I have taken up the motif for use in a woven carpet.

The story of the burning bush is one of several examples in the Old Testament telling of God's presence even though He remains invisible. He is present before Moses while the bush burns without being consumed, but Moses does not see Him; he hears His voice. In my new altar carpet I have treated this motif by placing the burning bush at the centre, almost in the form of a relief and surrounded by light. This light is further transformed into the darkness and blues of the heavens, surrounded by a circle of light that shines out to the altar rail and the congregation who on partaking of Holy Communion are gathered together for the essential moment when God and His Son are present.

The expression of the carpet also comes to resemble the heavens or an eye, God's eye. My deliberately subdued colours are consonant with the simplicity of the architecture and the colours in the body of the church. The reddish brown of the bricks is almost complementary to the bluish green of the altar carpet. The character of the altar carpet is only revealed when you approach that significant moment that the Eucharist represents for the communicant.

This work does not reproduce what is visible, but it makes visible.

THE BURNING BUSH
Woven altar carpet

132

THE BURNING BUSH
Detail and cartoon for the altar carpet
Chancel

QUEEN DAGMAR
South wall of the nave
Acrylic on canvas, 1998, 300 x 400 cm

134

GJELLERUP CHURCH

4 paintings set in a newly gilded altarpiece frame. Acrylic on canvas.
Stained glass, carved glass block and mouth-blown coloured glass.
Altar carpet, woven of wool, cotton, flax, silk and metal thread.
Pulpit, 5 reliefs with branches as motif in gilt hand-made plaster.
Gilt bronze dove above the pulpit. Newly gilded altar top.
Colour scheme for the entire church interior. Embellishment consecrated in 2007.
Architect: Lisbet Wolters.
Gilder: Ove Olsen. Stucco workers Brdr. Funder.
Glazier Per Steen Hebsgaard, Jannik Kvetny.
Weavers: Frédérique Bachellerie and Peter Schönewald, Atelier 3, Paris.
Bronze founders: Fonderia Marian i Pietra Santa.

Texts inspiring the embellishment
Central panel in the altarpiece: "Peace be unto you", John 20, 19,
Above the central panel: "The Holy Spirit", Acts 2, 1-13.
Stained glass: "The eyes of your understanding", Ephesians 1, 17-18.
Altar carpet: "The Burning Bush", Deuteronomy 4, 11-13.

EMBELLISHMENT OF GJELLERUP CHURCH

The altarpiece is finished off at the top of its external structure by a triangle in the best classical manner. As so often in Christian iconography, this triangle is also a symbol of the Trinity, which is to say the Father, the Son and the Holy Spirit. These are the very three elements that are so essential to the Christian faith. The space around the altar has been embellished with this in mind. (The triangle is found again on the tops of the pew ends). The Father is present in the altar carpet. The Son, Christ, stands out as the most important element in the central section of the altarpiece, envisaged walking in through the closed door to the congregation. The symbolical road, or way, is seen on both sides: the road to Emmaus or the Way, as Christ called Himself. (John 20, 19):

> *"Then the same day at evening, being the first day of the week, when the doors were shut where the disciples were assembled for fear of the Jews, came Jesus and stood in the midst, and saith unto them, Peace be unto you."*

Above the central panel there is a landscape to which I want to impart a heavenly light coming both from within and above. As an image of what it is most difficult to portray, that is to say the Holy Spirit.

Altarpiece prior to framing

Nave and chancel of the church

I regard the texts of the Old Testament as a foundation for the New Testament. I seek to emphasise this by making the motif in the altar carpet one from the Old Testament. That is to say that the altar rests on a foundation referring to the Old Testament. The motif in this carpet is the passage from Deuteronomy 4, 11-13, which runs:

"And ye came near and stood under the mountain; and the mountain burned with fire unto the midst of heaven, with darkness, clouds, and thick darkness. And the Lord spake unto you out of the midst of the fire: ye heard the voice of the words, but saw no similitude; only ye heard a voice. And he declared unto you his covenant, which he commanded you to perform, even ten commandments; and he wrote them upon two tablets of stone."

As always in the Old Testament, God is invisibly present. Sometimes symbolised by a burning bush, a pillar of cloud or an angel wrestling with Jacob. In this case, He is a burning mountain, almost, like the area that is surrounded by the altar rail and includes the altar carpet, separated off, as it says in Exodus 19, 12:

"And thou shalt set bounds unto the people round about, saying, Take heed to yourselves, that ye go not up into the mount, or touch the border of it."

My idea is to open up to the light pouring down on the burning mountain, the revealed Christ and the heavenly light in the image of the Holy Spirit. The window must stand there as a splintered chaos of light from which a heart with its eye emerges and merges into a point, (Ephesians 1, 17-18):

"That the God of our Lord Jesus Christ, the Father of glory, may give unto you the spirit of wisdom and revelation in the knowledge of him: The eyes of your understanding being enlightened; that ye may know what is the hope of his calling and what the riches of the glory of his inheritance in the saints."

In this way, the window with its light and symbol makes things more visible, dwelling in the eye of the heart. The pulpit with its simple motifs in the gilt panels is a point of light, the light that is seen again in the chancel. From where the text is preached and interpreted. Thus light is also visibly present.

THE BURNING MOUNTAIN
Altar and altar carpet

Detais from the church
Pulpit and stained glass to the south

142

HORNING CHURCH

Glass tessellae in the church's eastern niche above the altar.
Embellishment consecrated in 2007. Stucco workers. Brdr. Funder.

Text inspiring the embellishment
Motif in the niche: "The tree of life", John 15, 1-2.

My task of creating an embellishment behind the altar in Hørning Church was envisioned as a dialogue with the already existing gilt cross. Christ is portrayed here as both a cross and a figure with outstretched arms.

My idea was that I should recreate the heavenly light symbolised by the earlier east-facing Romanesque embrasures in the rear wall of the chancel. I did this not by literally opening the wall, but by dressing the existing hollow with golden mosaic tessellae in many shades of gold, like a starry sky or a gleaming flame. In this light-filled space I have put the tree of life, the tree of Jessica, the vine, the tree of the Cross, the tree from the Garden of Eden, a tree that draws its nourishment from the light and is surrounded by light. I have sought to depict all these trees, but primarily the tree of life.

In this way, the present single cross standing there has the light of the Resurrection and life behind it (John 15, 1-2):

"I am the true vine, and my Father is the husbandman. Every branch in me that beareth not fruit he taketh away and every branch that beareth fruit, he purgeth it, that it may bring forth more fruit."

Glass tessellae in the church's eastern
niche above the altar

Niche in the chancel
and details

TURUP CHURCH

Painting fitted in a newly gilded altar frame. Acrylic on canvas.
Colouring in the entire church interior.
The embellishment was consecrated in 2007.
Architect: Bendt Longmose Jakobsen, Clausen og Weber, Arkitekterne Svendborg.
Gilder: Ove Olsen.
The altar cloth created by the weaver Grethe Nielsen.

Text inspiring the embellishment
The motif in the altarpiece: "Jesus on the Shore", John 21, 4.

EMBELLISHMENT OF TURUP CHURCH

The motif in the altarpiece requires simplicity. Most of my New Testament paintings are centred on events in which the risen Christ is present. At first not recognised, as for instance in the three essential moments in St John's Gospel, at the beginning of Chapter 20, where He stands before Mary Magdalene, later in the chapter, when He reveals Himself to the disciples and especially Thomas, and at the beginning of John 21, 4, where it says:

"But when the morning was now come, Jesus stood on the shore: but the disciples knew not that it was Jesus."

It is this event that is the start of the miraculous catch of fish in the Sea of Galilee, which I have used in my motif for the altarpiece: the risen Christ standing alone on the lake shore, still not recognised by the disciples, on His way to give them and us His gift of love, an action that feeds our faith and hope. As emerges from the image, I have stressed the horizontal line of the coast and the vertical line of the figure, the shape of a cross, which refers to what has happened only in its form, but which in my altarpiece has put the cross behind it. Christ is reflected in the lake. The inscription above the altarpiece, "He has risen, He Lives" has been retained as have the other two texts above it.

The colour scheme is centred on shades of green: the luxuriance of the shore, the colour of the vine leaf, the olive leaves and the colours of the branches and the green of the Danish landscape.

Altarpiece before framing

Chancel and nave

VINDING CHURCH

Painting set in newly gilded altarpiece frame. Acrylic on canvas.
Colouring of the entire church interior.
Altar top in granite of different colours in collaboration with the architect.
The embellishment consecrated in 2008.
Architect Ebbe Lehn Petersen.
Gilder: Ove Olsen.

Text inspiring the embellishment
Altarpiece motif: "The Transfiguration", Matthew 17, 1-9.

EMBELLISHMENT OF VINDING CHURCH

A church with its surroundings and contents is like a living being. The place where we grew up leaves its mark on us, and the things we look at and have looked at every day influence us throughout our lives.

Vinding Church provides no exception to this idea either for history or for the congregation. The wonderful Romanesque granite sculpture portraying the surely sleeping and dreaming Jacob is so much a part of the church and so integrated in the attentive parishioner's memory that I from the start took my inspiration from its emanations and meaning. Like many of our old churches, this one stands on a hill – and Jacob is already here helped along in his dream up towards God.

There is another hill, a mountain in the New Testament that was my starting point for the altarpiece in this church. This is Mount Tabor, to which Christ goes with His three disciples Peter, James, and John, and in the text we find (Matthew 17, 1-8):

"And after six days Jesus taketh Peter, James and John his brother, and bringeth them up into an high mountain apart, And was transfigured before them: and his face did shine as the sun, and his raiment was white as the light. And behold, there appeared unto them Moses and Elias talking with him. Then answered Peter, and said unto Jesus, Lord it is good for us to be here: if thou wilt, let us make here three tabernacles; one for thee, and one for Moses, and one for Elias. While he yet spake, behold, a bright cloud overshadowed them; and behold a voice out of the cloud, which said, "This is my beloved Son, in whom I am well pleased; hear ye him." And when the disciples heard it, they fell on their face, and were sore afraid. And Jesus came and touched them, and said, Arise, and be not afraid. And when they had lifted up their eyes, they saw no man, save Jesus only. And as they came down from the mountain, Jesus charged them, saying, Tell the vision to no man until the Son of man be risen again from the dead."

Altarpiece before framing

153

This transfiguration on the mountain seems to me to suit the church for the reasons I give above. But it also fits in with the thoughts I have on church art in general. I try to portray Christ both as physically present, but also present in the light. I want to underline the presence of this light by gilding the dark sections of the altarpiece with a subdued layer of white gold and to retain the gilt of the existing altarpiece side by side with the new.

The altar top I have made in various shades of granite, a reference to the granite that is present in the two Romanesque figures decorating the outside of the church, the stone representing the sleeping Jacob and the bound figure.

Detail with romanesque granite sculptures
Chancel

155

MOU CHURCH

Altar cloth woven in wool, cotton, flax, silk and metal thread.
The altar surface in marble stucco.
The colouring of the entire body of the church.
Embellishment consecrated in 2008. Architect Søren Nørgaard, Plateau Arkitektur, Randers.
Weavers: Weavers: Frédérique Bachellerie and Peter Schönewald, Atelier 3, Paris.
Stucco workers: Brdr. Funder og Schiller.

Text inspiring the embellishment
Motif on the altar carpet: "The First Day", Genesis 1, 1-5.

EMBELLISHMENT OF MOU KIRKE

The altarpiece from 1582 is a Protestant triptych altar bearing the words of words of institution. It is powerful in its simplicity; the letters stand out graphically beautiful with their undulating and varied sizes. So it is very important that the altar should be simplified and presented in keeping with the old technique, marbled stucco, in a warm, brownish red shade.

The altar rail used to stand there as a barrier, almost a screen without any courtesy towards the kneeling communicant. But with the architect's new, simplified altar screen it is much friendlier, a place where the communicants can gather together.

During this central church ceremony the words of institution are reflected in the ceremony and the carpet that I have made for the space in front of the altar. For this reason, I chose a motif from the Old Testament inspired by the start of that Old Testament (Genesis 1, 1-5):

"In the beginning God created the heaven and the earth. And the earth was without form, and void; and darkness was upon the face of the deep. And the Spirit of God moved upon the face of the waters. And God said, Let there be light; and there was light. And God saw the light, that it was good; and God divided the light from the darkness. And God called the light Day, and the darkness he called Night. And the evening and the morning were the first day."

Thus there is on the floor a motif telling about the beginning of creation; mankind is still not present, and here the Word has not yet been heard, but everything is in embryo.

THE FIRST DAY
Altar carpet

In the Eucharist, Christianity has taken such a decisive step forward towards mankind and its salvation, of which the words of institution in the altarpiece so tellingly speak. The light and darkness and distance in the Old Testament are replaced by the New Testament message, of which the Eucharist – repeated every Sunday – is such a living sign. In this way, the two essential beginnings, that of the Earth and that of the Heavens in Genesis and the creation of the Word in the New Testament, the Word bearing the message of the Testament, are united before the altar and in the Eucharist.

The warm colours in the altar carpet are an extension of those in the altarpiece and harmonize with my choice of pale golden colours for the body of the church.

Detail of marble structure in the altar
and pews
Chancel

THE CHURCH ON STRANDVEJEN

One altarpiece, acrylic on canvas in a gilt frame with a relief of intertwined branches.
The embellishment consecrated in 2008. Gilder: Ove Olsen. Stucco workers: Brdr. Funder.

Text inspiring the embellishment
"I am the light of the world", *John 8, 12-13.*

THE EMBELLISHMENT OF THE CHURCH ON STRANDVEJEN

This is a light church containing for light in every sense of the word. So almost from the moment I stepped into it I was reminded of John 8, 12-13:

> *"Then spake Jesus again unto them, saying, I am the light of the world: he that followeth me shall not walk in darkness, but shall have the light of life. The Pharisees therefore said unto him, thou bearest record of thyself; thy record is not true."*

I have attempted to portray this light in my painting. When the Word from the Testaments is proclaimed, a new light is created, and if my painting only contains the light and radiates it, it comes from a light source different from that of light from the windows and the lamps and fills the church with a different dimension.

Behind the holy face, there stands a bare tree – a symbol of death that is now overcome, but which Christ himself has suffered. Thus, thanks to the many perpendicular lines His face is on its way away from the brownish darkness below to a shining, whitish light above. The indistinct face of the risen Christ means that His divine nature is now replacing His human nature.

But one day we shall see Him clearly, as it is put in Paul's uplifting prophecy (First Letter to the Corinthians 13, 12):

> *"For now we see through a glass, darkly; but then face to face; now I know in part; but then shall I know even as also I am known."*

Altarpiece before mounting in gilt
and modelled frame

160

Altarpiece in modelled gilt frame
Nave

LODBJERG CHURCH

2 side panels as bronze reliefs added to existing altarpiece and frame.
Pulpit: 5 painted panels. Acrylic on leather fixed to gilded wooden panels.
Colouring for the entire body of the church.
Embellishment consecrated in 2008.
Stucco workers: Brdr. Funder. Gilder: Ove Olsen. Foundry: Fonderia Mariani at Pietra Santa.

Texts omspiring the embellishment
Bronze reliefs when open:
Left panel: "The mark of the Risen Christ in the Darkness", low relief.
Right panel: "The mark of the Risen Christ in the Light", high relief.
When closed: "Jesus' Tomb Closed with a Stone at the Entrance".
The panels on the pulpit:
1. "The Star of Bethlehem", Matthew 2, 1-4.
2. "The Way", John 14, 6-8.
3. "The Face of Christ", Luke 24, 36-37.
4. "The Tree of Life", John 15, 1-9.
5. "Wings", Acts 2, 1-4.

EMBELLISHMENT OF LODBJERG CHURCH

The existing painted motif on the altarpiece on the high altar is Christ surrounded for the Last Supper by His disciples the day before Good Friday, and the two side panels are made in bronze with the risen Christ in relief. The closed triptych is like the closed tomb after Christ was laid there, with a motif in bronze of the stone that has been placed before the tomb.

As a modern artist, it is difficult to enter into a dialogue with an old altarpiece, which in its naive honesty and rather clumsy finish nevertheless has the simplicity of faith about it. So I decided in my proposal not add a painting, but a motif reflecting the expression of light.

The left panel is a relief of the same figure as that in the right panel. The central altarpiece itself represents the institution of the Eucharist with the burial and resurrection in its side panels. Symbolically and figuratively, the left panel represents the empty tomb on Easter Morning, with only the shadow remaining of the risen Christ who in the right panel is seen by the congregation as a radiant figure.

Instead of absorbing the light, the altarpiece will now emit light. And my entire wish to give fresh light to the church is fulfilled.

Altarpiece

164

JEG ER LIVETS BRØD.   JEG ER VERDENS LYS.

JOH. 6, 48.   JOH. 8, 12.

Altarpiece closed
Chancel

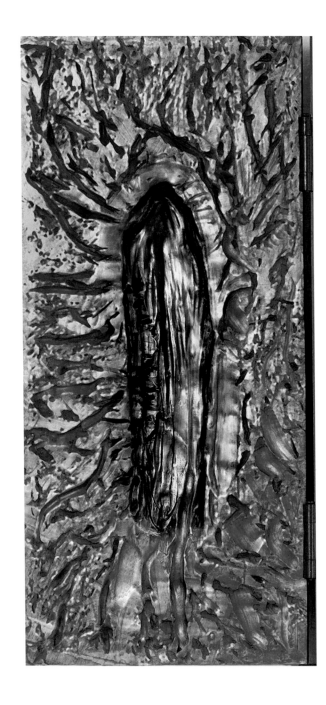

Altarpiece
Open side panel
Nave with chancel arch

168

I have also modified the pulpit partly with colour and partly by adding five paintings on a gilt background. Each painting is executed on a separate plate and mounted on the gilt background. The gilding in the pulpit harmonises with the gilding in the altar. The gold, which symbolically has both the light and thus Christ hidden within it, also has the ability to reflect. As this is a small church, everything will be opened up as a result of the reflection.

Matthew 2, 1-4
"Now when Jesus was born in Bethlehem of Judæa in the days of Herod the king, behold, there came wise men from the east to Jerusalem, saying, Where is he that is born King of the Jews? For we have seen his star in the east, and are come to worship him. When Herod the king had heard these things, he was troubled, and all Jerusalem with him. And when he had gathered all the chief priests and scribes of the people together, he demanded of them where Christ should be born."

John 14, 6-8

"Jesus saith unto him, I am the way, the truth and the life: no man cometh unto the Father, but by me. If ye had known me, ye should have known my Father also: and from henceforth ye know him and have seen him. Philip saith unto him, Lord, shew us the Father, and it sufficeth us."

Luke 24, 36-37
"And as they thus spake, Jesus himself stood in the midst of them, and saith unto them, Peace be unto you.
But they were terrified and affrighted, and supposed that they had seen a spirit."

John 15, 1-9

"I am the true vine, and my Father is the husbandman. Every branch in me that beareth not fruit he taketh away, and every branch that beareth fruit, he purgeth it, that it may bring forth more fruit. Now ye are clean through the word which I have spoken unto you. Abide in me, and I in you. As the branch cannot bear fruit of itself, except it abide in the vine; no more can ye, except ye abide in me. I am the vine, ye are the branches: He that abideth in me, and I in him, the same bringeth forth much fruit: for without me ye can do nothing. If a man abide not in me, he is cast forth as a branch, and is withered; and men gather them and cast them into the fire, and they are burned. If ye abide in me, and my words abide in you, ye shall ask what ye will, and it shall be done unto you. Herein is my Father glorified, that ye bear much fruit; so shall ye be my disciples. As the Father hath loved me, so have I loved you: continue ye in my love."

Acts 2, 1-4

"And when the day of Pentecost was fully come, they were all with one accord in one place. And suddenly there came a sound from heaven as of a rushing mighty wind, and it filled all the house where they were sitting. And there appeared unto them cloven tongues like as of fire, and it sat upon each of them. And they were all filled with the Holy Ghost, and began to speak with other tongues, as the Spirit gave them utterance."

RAKLEV CHURCH

Stained glass in the south side of the nave, a painted sheet with motif burned in the glass, a sheet of cut, mouth-blown coloured glass. Colouring for the entire church interior.
The embellishment consecrated in 2010. Architect: Erik Sørensen MAA, Brøgger Arkitektfirma A/S.
Glaziers: Per Steen Hebsgaard, Jannik Kvetny.

Text that inspired the embellisment
The motif in the glass mosaic: "The Good Shepherd", John 10, 9.

EMBELLISHMENT OF RAKLEV CHURCH

Raklev Church is one of those churches that stand on an elevated point in the landscape – it can be seen from the Sejrø Bay, and conversely there is an extensive view from the church.

I personally feel a close association with the church; it was here my sisters and I were both baptised and confirmed; my first school was Raklev Central School, and from our home in Svenstrup near the coast at Vrøj I cycled in all kinds of weather, first through the flat landscape and then up towards Raklev. The church always stood as a focal point in the landscape.

I soon had the idea of making a stained glass window in the south wall near the door through which you leave the church. The text that inspired me to a motif based on "The Good Shepherd" runs (John 10, 9):

"I am the door; by me if any man enter in, he shall be saved, and shall go in and out, and find pasture."

One characteristic feature of a stained glass window is that it contains a motif between indoors and outdoors, between light and darkness, between tangible and intangible; the pane is like a door, and so I have fashioned my motif in such a way that it is also a reference to the text. The figure of Christ goes in and out over the green pastures in the window, but thanks to His transparency, He is at the same time a spiritual opening through which the visitor to the church can pass.

The faint picture that the light passing through the glass will project on to the whitewashed wall opposite will vary with the changing light of each season, tinted by the blues and greens in the mosaic. Colours that are taken from my childhood experiences on the way to Raklev.

Stained glass
to the south

176

177

178

Stained glass and detail
Nave

Eight stained glass windows in the church. A painted sheet with motif burned in the glass, a sheet of cut, mouth-blown stained glass.
The first stained glass window in the north side consecrated in 2007.
The remaining seven widows in the south side were consecrated in 2010.
Glaziers: Per Steen Hebsgard, Jannik Kvetny.

Texts inspiring the embellishment
North window: "Angel Wings", Acts 2, 1-4.
South windows: "The Seven Days of Creation", Genesis 1, 1-31 & 2, 1-4.

EMBELLISHMENT OF ST MARY'S CHURCH, LIOBA CONVENT

The shape of the angel is characteristic mainly due to its being a winged human-like figure. And what an important messenger the angel is. In the Old Testament, Abraham is visited by three angels who tell him of the event that made his wife Sara laugh when she heard that she was to give birth to a child, the future patriarch Isaac. Elsewhere in the Bible, Jacob wrestles throughout an entire night with the angel who finally blesses him. In the New Testament Mary is informed of the birth of the coming Saviour by an angelic messenger. The Holy Spirit in the form of a dove is also by its very nature a winged messenger.

I have used the wings of this angel and the wings of the Holy Spirit as my principal motif in the stained glass window to the north. Partly because its symbol is a joyful message, and partly because the thoughts and deeds of St Lioba spread throughout Europe as though they were dispatched on wings. In its very shape, the tall window with its upward sweep almost betokens a wing bringing light from above. In contrast to a painting on a wall or in an altarpiece, the character of the stained glass window is that, while walls and altarpieces have light thrown on them, the stained glass window radiates light by having the light passing through it. By its very nature, this transcendence is close to the entire symbolism of the presence of Christ and the Holy Spirit as light.

The angel's wing is related to the text (Acts 2, 1-4):

"And when the day of Pentecost was fully come, they were all with one accord in one place. And suddenly there came a sound from heaven as of a rushing mighty wind, and it filled all the house where they were sitting. And there appeared unto them cloven tongues like as of fire, and it sat upon each of them. And they were all filled with the Holy Ghost, and began to speak with other tongues, as the Spirit gave them utterance."

Stained glass
to the north

180

At one time it struck me as natural that I should introduce the seven west windows in the church in such a way as to form an embellishment containing new stained glass. Hidden in the number seven there are many symbols linked to Christianity, but it quickly became clear to me that the content of the windows must be the story of the Creation based on the Old Testament text in Genesis.

At that time I was engaged on doing a number of paintings which over recent years have been shown in three exhibitions, entitled "The First Day", "The Second Day" and "The Third Day".

As an artist, I have found it quite natural to work with the Creation as a motif. I feel that the essence of an artist's work is constantly to ask questions about the mystery of Creation. When you stand before a blank canvas, nothing has yet started; the theory of perspective has not yet been invented, up and down, large and small, form and shadow, light and darkness, none of the elements that play their part in giving a painting an expression, have yet been registered or fixed. In all humility I feel the presence of this blank canvas as the start of things that is so powerfully described in the text in Genesis. It seems to me to be natural as a painter to use this text as a guiding principle for all creation, and I have decided through the medium of seven exhibitions to follow the Genesis text through to the blessing and the day of rest.

The ancient Greeks, especially Plato, believed that the reality surrounding us should be reproduced artistically as precisely as possible; you must copy reality. To Plato, a work of art could only reproduce a presence that already existed. The artists' own creative imagination was not accepted. Mimed reality shows what is seen, while the imagination shows what is not seen.

In the story of Creation and to my mind, the creation of a work of art is not compatible with Plato's theories. One new concept – faith – must be introduced and added to the artist's imagination and ability. The whole of St Augustine's thought that "It was far too late I learned to love You, God; You were inside, but I was outside; You were with me, but I was not with You" clearly tells of the conflict there was between the logic and clarity of Greek thought and the light that a new thought borne on faith brought into the world via the Star of Bethlehem.

By virtue of the technique I have chosen, that is to say stained glass, working with the Creation in the seven windows for the church receives a further powerful dimension in that these works of art live and die with the coming and going of light. This tidal dimension of light, this interplay from morning to evening has so much to do with the entire flow of the text in Genesis. Making the windows part of the body of the church, establishes a union between the life of the church and the Christian text relating the story of the Creation.

Nave to the south

182

"In the beginning God created the heaven and the earth. And the earth was without form, and void; and darkness was upon the face of the deep. And the Spirit of God moved upon the face of the waters. And God said, Let there be light: and there was light."

184

"And God said, Let there be a firmament in the midst of the waters, and let it divide the waters from the waters. And God made the firmament, and divided the waters which were under the firmament from the waters which were above the firmament: and it was so. And God called the firmament Heaven. And the evening and the morning were the second day."

186

THE THIRD DAY

"And God said: Let the waters under the heaven be gathered together unto one place, and let the dry land appear: and it was so. And God called the dry land Earth; and the gathering together of the waters called he seas: and God saw that it was good. And God said, Let the earth bring forth grass, the herb yielding seed, and the fruit tree yielding fruit after his kind, whose seed is in itself, upon the earth; and it was so."

THE FOURTH DAY
"And God said: Let there be lights in the firmament of the heaven to divide the day from the night; and he let them be for signs, and for seasons, and for days, and years. And let them be for lights in the firmament of the heaven to give light upon the earth: and it was so."

THE FIFTH DAY

"God said: Let the waters bring forth abundantly the moving creature that hath life, and fowl that may fly above the earth in the open firmament of heaven. And God created great whales, and every living creature that moveth, which the waters brought forth abundantly after their kind, and every winged fowl after his kind: and God saw that it was good. And God blessed them, saying, Be fruitful, and multiply, and fill the waters in the seas, and let fowl multiply in the earth."

THE SIXTH DAY
"So God crated man in his own image, in the image of God created he him; male
and female created he them."

THE SEVENTH DAY

"Thus the heavens and the earth were finished, and all the host of them. And on the seventh day God ended his work, which he had made; and he rested on the seventh day from all his work which he had made."

FARSØ CHURCH

Altarpiece in the form of a triptych, 3 paintings in a freshly gilded frame. Acrylic on canvas.
2 side panels and tympanum: reliefs in 24 carat gilt hard plaster.
Pulpit: 5 reliefs in 24 carat gilt hard plaster.
Predella panel with carved text in gilt wood.
Colour scheme for the entire body of the church.
The embellishment was consecrated in 2010.
Architect: Erik Sørensen, MAA, KS Arkitekter.
Gilder: Ove Olsen. Stucco workers: Brdr. Funder.

Texts inspiring the embellishment
Altarpiece open: "The Promise of the Holy Spirit", Acts 1, 7-9.
Altarpiece closed: "The curtain is torn", Luke 23, 44-47.
The open hard plaster side panel, tympanum and pulpit panels are all based on themes concerning the "wings of the Holy Spirit".

EMBELLISHMENT OF FARØ CHURCH

The most powerful and characteristic works of art in Farø Church are the tympanum above the north door and the font, both decorated with lion motifs.

It is generally accepted that these two important granite works were made by the same master. Without wishing to embark on a discussion of the manifold symbolical power of the lions, I would nevertheless like to emphasise one symbol represented by them, that is to say the family of David, the king of the Israelites.

This persuaded me to establish an indirect link to the motif in my altarpiece, in which I wanted to have Christ at the centre. Christ was a member of David's family.

Christianity has left its traces in so many places that one is inclined to forget the origins of such and such a ritual. Even a town hall wedding requires two witnesses, and I could point to many other Old Testament rules that more or less consciously form the basis of many everyday acts. This dualism, the two witnesses, this duality is also to be seen in the granite lions in the church, which are two bodies and one head.

The same duality is characteristic of a triptych, in which there are two panels that can be opened and closed around the central image that stands in the middle of the altar. With my proposal and choice I also wish to point out the presence in the church at the same time of the two Romanesque works in granite.

Altarpiece before installation
in frame

199

But primarily I wanted to create an independent work, an altarpiece with its point of departure in a motif that starts out in what for me is an important fundamental feature in the church embellishments I have carried out so far, that is to say the risen Christ. The Ascension is the backbone of Christianity as a whole, but it is impossible to conceive of it without seeing the suffering and the death that preceded it.

According to tradition, a triptych altarpiece is closed about Maundy Thursday or Good Friday and is first opened again like the stone that is moved from the tomb on Easter Morning. While it is closed, all that is seen is the outside of the two panels, adorned with a painting that takes its inspiration from the following text (Luke 23, 44-47):

"And it was about the sixth hour, and there was a darkness over all the earth until the ninth hour. And the sun was darkened, and the veil of the temple was rent in the midst. And when Jesus had cried with a loud voice, he said, Father, into thy hands I commend my spirit: and having said thus, he gave up the ghost."

On Easter Day, the panels and the grave are opened during divine service. With the resurrection, all sorrow and despair are gone. My principal motif on the open panel is taken from Acts 1, 3-8:

"To whom also he shewed himself alive after his passion by many infallible proofs, being seen of them forty days, and speaking of the things pertaining to the kingdom of God: And, being assembled together with them, commanded them that they should not depart from Jerusalem, but wait for the promise of the Father, which, saith he, ye have heard of me. For John truly baptized with water; but ye shall be baptized with the Holy Ghost not many days hence. When they therefore were come together, they asked of him, saying, Lord, wilt though at this time restore again the kingdom to Israel. And he said unto them, It is not for you to know the times or the seasons, which the Father hath put in his own power. But ye shall receive power after that the Holy Ghost is come upon you: and ye shall be witnesses unto me both in Jerusalem, and in all Judæa, and in Samaria, and unto the uttermost part of the earth.

This important passage introduces Whitsuntide and the thought of the presence of the Holy Spirit. With the portrayal of the figure of Christ and with the light dwelling within Him, I attempt to express the inexplicable power and the promise that the heralding of the Holy Spirit represents.

The two side panels meet with Christ in the centre panel, like the bodies of the two lions in the granites, and the motifs in the panels represent a pair of wings as the bearers and messengers of the Holy Spirit. They are in the form of a tongue of fire.

Altarpiece before installation
in frame

200

Nave with the closed
and open altarpiece
Nave pp. 204-205

202

203

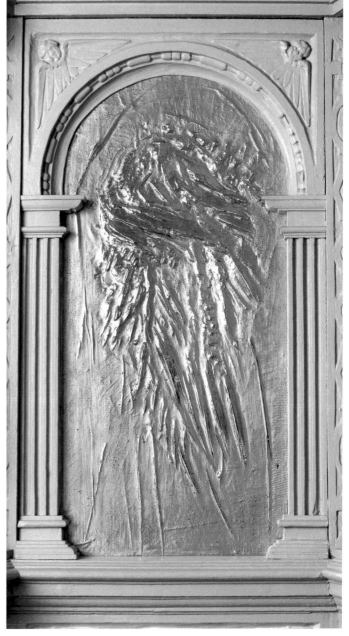

Pulpit
Pulpit with details

OVERVIEW OF CHURCHES

1
ØSTER TØRSLEV CHURCH
Kirkevej 1B
Øster Tørslev
8983 Gjerlev J
www.sogn.dk/oestertoerslev

2
SKELUND CHURCH
Teglbakkevej 3
Skelund
9560 Hadsund
www.skelundkirke.dk

3
GRINDERSLEV CHURCH
Klostervej 29
Breum
7870 Roslev
www.grinderslevkirke.dk

4
HOLSTED CHURCH
Holsted Allé 1
4700 Næstved
www.holstedkirke.folkekirken.dk

5
HYLLEHOLT CHURCH
Hovedgaden 13C
4654 Fakse Ladeplads
www.tryggevaeldeprovsti.dk

6
KULLERUP CHURCH
Ferritslevvej 28
5853 Ørbæk
www.kullerupkirke.dk

7
FREDERIKS CHURCH
Nørregade 52
Frederiks
7470 Karup J
www.frederikssogn.dk

8
STOENSE CHURCH
Stoensevej 22A
5953 Tranekær
www.sogn.dk/stoense

9
SKANNERUP CHURCH
Hammelvej 6
8883 Gjern
www.sogn.dk/skannerup

10
ST CATHERINE'S CHURCH
Sct. Catharinæ Plads 1
6760 Ribe
www.sct-catharinae.dk

11
GJELLERUP CHURCH
Kirkebyvej 1
7400 Herning
www.gjellerupkirke.dk

12
HØRNING CHURCH
Nørre Alle 6
8362 Hørning.
www.hoerning.folkekirken.dk

13
TURUP CHURCH
Gamtoftevej 90
5610 Assens
www.sogn.dk/turup

14
VINDING CHURCH
Vindingvej 94
7100 Vejle
www.vindingkirkevejle.dk

15
MOU CHURCH
Dokkedalvej 8a
Mou
9280 Storvorde
www.mousogn.dk

16
THE CHURCH ON STRANDEJEN
Humlebæk Strandvej 54
3050 Humlebæk
www.strandvejskirken.dk

17
LODBJERG CHURCH
Lodbjerg Kirkevej 1
7770 Vestervig
www.sogn.dk/lodbjerg

18
RAKLEV CHURCH
Raklev Skillevej 2A
4400 Kalundborg
www.raklevkirke.dk

19
ST MARY'S CHURCH
Jens Jessensvej 5-7
2000 Frederiksberg
www.mariae.dk

20
FARSØ CHURCH
Nørregade
9640 Farsø
www.farsoe.folkekirken.dk

BIOGRAPHY

1956	Maja Lisa Engelhardt born at Frederiksberg
1978-1980	Funen Academy of Art
1985	First exhibition, Nikolaj Kirke, (St Nicholas' Church) Copenhagen
1989	Prins Henriks Legat
1988	Rockwool Prize
1998	Tagea Brandt's Travelling Bursary
1999	Nordic First Prize for colouring of Roskilde Museum
2001	Member of Corner
2003	Artist of the Year, Kunstavisen
2010	Kristeligt Dagblad Prize
	Permanent association with Galleri Weinberger, Copenhagen and the Elisabeth Harris Gallery, New York

PUBLIC COMMISIONS

Søren Kierkegaard Research Centre, Copenhagen
Social Democrat Group chambers, Christiansborg (Danish Parliament)
Nykredit, Head office, Copenhagen
Coloplast, Espergærde
Odense Town Hall
Supreme Court, Copenhagen
Frederiksberg Court
Deloitte, Copenhagen
C.W. Obel, Copenhagen
Office of the Parliamentary Commissioner, Copenhagen
Ikast Training College
Royal Danish Academy of Sciences and Letters
Faculty of Theology, Copenhagen University
Tivoli Concert House, Copenhagen
Grenå Municipal High School
Danmarks Radio, Copenhagen
Copenhagen University
Roskilde University Library
Nordea Danmark Foundation, Copenhagen
Danish Agricultural Advisory Council Main Offices, Copenhagen
National Telecom Agency, Copenhagen
Tele Danmark Head Office, Copenhagen
Ecco Center, Tønder
Rigshospitalet, Copenhagen
Copenhagen City Court
Jyske Bank Head Office, Silkeborg
Royal Veterinary and Agricultural University
Hospice Sjælland, Roskilde
Hospicegården, Dianalund
Nynäs Oil, Sweden
Århus University
Sanatorium for Rheumatic Diseases, Skælskør

BIBLIOGRAPHY

1985   *Klædebon* (Raiment). Exhibition catalogue with reproductions
        Text: Lise Funder. Nikolaj Church, Copenhagen

1986   *Illuminations*. Exhibition catalogue with reproductions
        Text: Marcel Monnies. Brandts Pakhus, Copenhagen

1988   *Tornekrone* (Crown of Thorns). Exhibition catalogue with reproductions
        Text: Hans Edvard Nørregård-Nielsen. Gallery Weinberger, Copenhagen

1990   *Prøvetryk* (Trial Proofs). Exhibition catalogue with reproductions
        Text: Maja Lisa Engelhardt. Gallery Weinberger, Copenhagen

1991   *Eg-Skejten* (Oak-Skejten). Illustrated by Maja Lisa Engelhardt
        Text: Johannes V. Jensen. Boggalleriet, Rønde, Denmark
        Efter naturen (After Nature). Exhibition catalogue with reproductions
        Text: Henrik Wivel. Sophienholm, Lyngby, Denmark

1992   *Landscape Fragments*. Diary entries, Paintings, Photography, Sketches
        Text: Flemming Friborg. Forlaget Privattryk, Danish and English edition

1993   *10 lithographs*. Catalogue with introduction and reproductions
        Edition Yann Samson. Paris-Colombes

1994   *Mark* (Field). Illustrated by Maja Lisa Engelhardt
        Text: Martin A. Hansen. Boggalleriet, Rønde, Denmark

1995   *Weilbach's Encyclopedia of Art*
        Text Hanne Abildgaard. Weilbach, Copenhagen
        Tumulus. Exhibition catalogue with reproductions
        Text: Henrik Wivel. D.C.A. Gallery, New York
        N.Y. 1995 Monotypes. Book with reproductions
        Text: Hans Edvard Nørregård-Nielsen. Poem by Seamus Heaney. Knudtzons Bogtrykkeri, Copenhagen

1996   *Burning Bush*. Exhibition catalogue with reproductions
        Text: David Carrier. D.C.A. Gallery, New York

1997   *Sø* (Lake). Exhibition catalogue with reproductions
        Text: Maja Lisa Engelhardt, diary notes. Gallery Weinberger, Copenhagen

1998   *Vinger I-XX* (Wings I-XX). Book with reproductions
        Poem by Pär Lagerkvist. Gallery Weinberger

1999   *Jakobs kamp med englen* (Jacob's Fight with the Angel). Book with reproductions
        Text: Henrik Wivel and Bent Melchior. Gallery Weinberger, Copenhagen

2000   *Light/Darkness. Way through Landscape*. Exhibition catalogue with reproductions
        Text: Lisbeth Smedegaard-Andersen. D.C.A. Gallery, New York
        Way through Landscape.
        Text: Jeremy Gilbert-Rolfe
        The Melancholy Figure
        Text: Flemming Friborg. Book with reproductions. Ny Carlsberg Glyptotek, Copenhagen
        Saxo – The History of Denmark. Books with reproductions
        Text translated from Latin: Peter Zeeberg, Gads Forlag and D.S.L.
2001   *Ridderen fra Danmark* (The Knight from Denmark). Illustrated by Maja Lisa Engelhardt
        Text: Sophia de mello Breyner Andresen. Forlaget Rhodos
2002   *Usynlig til synlig* (Invisible to Visible). Exhibition catalogue with reproductions
        Text: Lisbeth Smedegaard Andersen. Museet Holmen, Løgumkloster
        A Monograph Book with reproductions
        Text: Henrik Wivel. D.C.A. Gallery, New York
2003   *Pillar of a Cloud*. Book and exhibition cataloque with reproductions
        Text: Maja Lisa Engelhardt. D.C.A. Gallery, New York
2004   *Åbenbaret* (Revealed). Book and exhibition cataloque with reproductions
        Texts: Hans Edvard Nørregård-Nielsen, Nils Ohrt, Dagmar Warming and Sandra Kastfelt
2005   *Hviskende brise*. (Whispering Wind)
        Text, Poems by: H.R.H. Prince Henrik of Denmark
        Illustrated by: Maja Lisa Engelhardt
        Poul Kristensens Forlag
        Burning Bush. A Tapistry to Sct. Catharinae Church, Ribe. Book with reproductions
        Text: Jørgen Bork Hansen
2006   *Aftenland* (Land of Evenings) Poems by Pär Lagerkvist
        Illustrated by Maja Lisa Engelhardt. Text: Henrik Wivel.
        Aftonland (Land of Evenings). Kabusa Böcker, Göteborg. 2007
        Landscape, Autumn. Five reliefs in bronze. Text by Flemming Friborg
        with reproductions. Brødrene Funder, Copenhagen

2007   *The Second Day*. Catalogue with reproductions and text by the artist
Elizabeth Harris Gallery, New York
Tilstedeværelse (Presence). Catalogue with reproductions
Text: Nils Ohrt. Museum Sønderjylland, Haderslev

2008   *B.S. Ingemann: Morgen- og Aftensange* (Songs for Morning and Evening)
Illustrated by Maja Lisa Engelhardt
Text: Niels Kofoed. Published by Gyldendal, Copenhagen
Himlens lys i dine hænder (Heavenly Light in your Hands)
Text: Lisbeth Smedegaard-Andersen. Illustrated by Maja Lisa Engelhardt
Published by Anis, Copenhagen

2009   *The Third Day*. Exhibition catalogue with reproductions
Text: Maja Lisa Engelhardt
Elizabeth Harris Gallery, New York

2010   Søren Kierkegaard: *Liljen på Marken og Fuglen under Himmelen*
Illustrations: Maja Lisa Engelhardt.
Afterword: Niels Jørgen Cappelørn. Kristeligt Dagblads Forlag
Fri hjul. Poems by His Royal Highness Prince Henrik
Illustrations: Her Majesty Queen Margrethe and Maja Lisa Engelhardt. Poul Kristensens Forlag

SOLO EXHIBITIONS

1985   *Klædebon* (Raiment). Debut exhibition, Nikolaj Church, Copenhagen

1986   *Illuminations*, Brandts Pakhus, Copenhagen

1988   *Tornekrone* (Crown of Thorns). Gallery Weinberger, Copenhagen

1989   *Kornaks over landskab* (Ears of Corn over Landscape). Århus Municipal Hospital, Århus, Denmark

           Plov i landskab (Plough in Landscape). Politiken Foyer, Copenhagen (in connection with the publication of a special graphic print by the artist and the newspaper)

1990   Aalborg Historical Museum, Aalborg, Denmark

           Prøvetryk (Trial Proofs). Gallery Weinberger, Copenhagen

1991   *Efter Naturen* (After Nature). Sophienholm, Lyngby, Denmark

           Eg-Skejten (Oak-Skejten). Gallery Weinberger, Copenhagen

1992   *Landskabsfragmenter* (Landscape Fragments). Bishop's Palace, Kalundborg, Denmark

1993   *Mark, Landskabsfragmenter* (Field, Landscape Fragments). Gallery Weinberger, Copenhagen

1995   *Tumulus*. D.C.A. Gallery, New York

           Gravhøje (Burial Mounds). Swedish Villa, Bernstorff Castle Park, Copenhagen

1996   *Burning Bush*. D.C.A. Gallery, New York

1997   *Sø* (Lake). Gallery Weinberger, Copenhagen. *Sø* (Lake) Galleri Profilen, Århus

2000   *Light/Darkness, Way through Landscape*. D.C.A. Gallery, New York

           Vej gennem landskab (Way through Landscape). The New Carlsberg Glyptotek, Copenhagen

           Vej gennem landskab (Way through Landscape). Gallery Weinberger, Copenhagen

2002   *Usynlig til synlig* (Invisible to Visible). Museet Holmen, Løgumkloster

2003   *Pillar of a Cloud*. D.C.A. Gallery, New York

2004   *Bølgebrud* (Breaking the Waves). Gallery Weinberger, Copenhagen

           Åbenbaret (Revealed) Museet for Religiøs Kunst, Lemvig, Nivaagaards Malerisamling, Kunsthallen, Brandts Klædefabrik, all Denmark

2006   *The First Day*. Gallery Weinberger, Copenhagen

2007   *The Second Day*, Elizabeth Harris Gallery, New York

           Tilstedeværelse (Presence), Museum Sønderjylland, Haderslev, Denmark

2009   *Ingemann monotypier* (Monotypes to Ingemann), Gallery Weinberger, Copenhagen

           The Third Day. Elizabeth Harris Gallery, New York

2010   *En rose så jeg skyde* (Lo' how a rose e'er blooming). Paintings

           Søren Kierkegaard's *Liljen på Marken og Fuglen under Himmelen* (The Lily of the Field and the Bird under the Sky). Monotypes. Gallery Weinberger, Copenhagen

CONTENTS

TOWARDS THE LIGHT

© Maja Lisa Engelhard Else Marie Bukdahl, Claus Grymer
and Kristeligt Dagblads Forlag 2011
Photos from the Churches: Leif Tuxen
Studiophotos: Knud Sejersen, Inferno
Layout: Maja Lisa Engelhardt
1st edition. 1st printing
Cover: Motif of stained glass from Grinderslev Church
The book is composed with Goudy Oldstyle 12/16
and printed on 150 g Hello Fat mat 1.1
Printed by Narayana Press, Gylling
Bound by Thomas Müntzer, Germany
Translation: Glyn Jones

ISBN 978-87-9098-025-2

The book is published with kind support from:
Ny Carlsbergfondet
Aage og Johanne Louis-Hansens Fond
Stryhn Holding

www.k.dk/forlag

*The Farsø Church embellisment was finished too late to be visited
and commented by Else Marie Bukdahl.*